OPPOSING
VIEWPOINTS®
SERIES

| Racial Profiling

Other Books of Related Interest:

Opposing Viewpoints Series
Criminal Justice
Civil Liberties
US Airport Security

At Issue Series
Does the World Hate the United States?
Mexico's Drug Wars
Should the United States Close Its Borders?

Current Controversies Series
Developing Nations
Human Trafficking
Islamophobia

"Congress shall make no law . . . abridging the freedom of speech, or of the press."

First Amendment to the US Constitution

The basic foundation of our democracy is the First Amendment guarantee of freedom of expression. The Opposing Viewpoints series is dedicated to the concept of this basic freedom and the idea that it is more important to practice it than to enshrine it.

| Racial Profiling

Carol Ullmann and Lynn M. Zott, Book Editors

GREENHAVEN PRESS

A part of Gale, Cengage Learning

Detroit • New York • San Francisco • New Haven, Conn • Waterville, Maine • London

GALE
CENGAGE Learning·

Elizabeth Des Chenes, *Director, Publishing Solutions*

© 2013 Greenhaven Press, a part of Gale, Cengage Learning.
Gale and Greenhaven Press are registered trademarks used herein under license.

For more information, contact:
Greenhaven Press
27500 Drake Rd.
Farmington Hills, MI 48331-3535
Or you can visit our Internet site at gale.cengage.com

For product information and technology assistance, contact us at

Gale Customer Support, 1-800-877-4253
For permission to use material from this text or product, submit all requests online at www.cengage.com/permissions

Further permissions questions can be emailed to permissionrequest@cengage.com

Articles in Greenhaven Press anthologies are often edited for length to meet page require-ments. In addition, original titles of these works are changed to clearly present the main thesis and to explicitly indicate the author's opinion. Every effort is made to ensure that Greenhaven Press accurately reflects the original intent of the authors. Every effort has been made to trace the owners of copyrighted material.

Cover Image copyright © Zurijeta/Shutterstock.com.

LIBRARY OF CONGRESS CATALOGING-IN-PUBLICATION DATA

Racial profiling / Carol Ullmann and Lynn M. Zott, book editors.
    pages cm. -- (Opposing viewpoints)
    Includes bibliographical references and index.
    ISBN 978-0-7377-6070-5 (hardcover) -- ISBN 978-0-7377-6071-2 (pbk.)
    1. Racial profiling in law enforcement--United States--Juvenile literature. I. Ull-
mann, Carol. II. Zott, Lynn M. (Lynn Marie), 1969-
    HV7936.R3R326 2013
    363.25'8--dc23
                                                                2012045999

Printed in the United States of America
1 2 3 4 5 6 7 17 16 15 14 13

Contents

Chapter 4: What Are the Consequences of Racial Profiling?

Why Consider Opposing Viewpoints?

> "The only way in which a human being can make some approach to knowing the whole of a subject is by hearing what can be said about it by persons of every variety of opinion and studying all modes in which it can be looked at by every character of mind. No wise man ever acquired his wisdom in any mode but this."
>
> *John Stuart Mill*

In our media-intensive culture it is not difficult to find differing opinions. Thousands of newspapers and magazines and dozens of radio and television talk shows resound with differing points of view. The difficulty lies in deciding which opinion to agree with and which "experts" seem the most credible. The more inundated we become with differing opinions and claims, the more essential it is to hone critical reading and thinking skills to evaluate these ideas. Opposing Viewpoints books address this problem directly by presenting stimulating debates that can be used to enhance and teach these skills. The varied opinions contained in each book examine many different aspects of a single issue. While examining these conveniently edited opposing views, readers can develop critical thinking skills such as the ability to compare and contrast authors' credibility, facts, argumentation styles, use of persuasive techniques, and other stylistic tools. In short, the Opposing Viewpoints Series is an ideal way to attain the higher-level thinking and reading skills so essential in a culture of diverse and contradictory opinions.

In addition to providing a tool for critical thinking, Opposing Viewpoints books challenge readers to question their own strongly held opinions and assumptions. Most people form their opinions on the basis of upbringing, peer pressure, and personal, cultural, or professional bias. By reading carefully balanced opposing views, readers must directly confront new ideas as well as the opinions of those with whom they disagree. This is not to argue simplistically that everyone who reads opposing views will—or should—change his or her opinion. Instead, the series enhances readers' understanding of their own views by encouraging confrontation with opposing ideas. Careful examination of others' views can lead to the readers' understanding of the logical inconsistencies in their own opinions, perspective on why they hold an opinion, and the consideration of the possibility that their opinion requires further evaluation.

Evaluating Other Opinions

To ensure that this type of examination occurs, Opposing Viewpoints books present all types of opinions. Prominent spokespeople on different sides of each issue as well as well-known professionals from many disciplines challenge the reader. An additional goal of the series is to provide a forum for other, less known, or even unpopular viewpoints. The opinion of an ordinary person who has had to make the decision to cut off life support from a terminally ill relative, for example, may be just as valuable and provide just as much insight as a medical ethicist's professional opinion. The editors have two additional purposes in including these less known views. One, the editors encourage readers to respect others' opinions—even when not enhanced by professional credibility. It is only by reading or listening to and objectively evaluating others' ideas that one can determine whether they are worthy of consideration. Two, the inclusion of such viewpoints encourages the important critical thinking skill of objectively evaluating an author's credentials and bias. This evaluation will illuminate an author's reasons for taking a particular stance on an issue and will aid in readers' evaluation of the author's ideas.

It is our hope that these books will give readers a deeper understanding of the issues debated and an appreciation of the complexity of even seemingly simple issues when good and honest people disagree. This awareness is particularly important in a democratic society such as ours in which people enter into public debate to determine the common good. Those with whom one disagrees should not be regarded as enemies but rather as people whose views deserve careful examination and may shed light on one's own.

Thomas Jefferson once said that "difference of opinion leads to inquiry, and inquiry to truth." Jefferson, a broadly educated man, argued that "if a nation expects to be ignorant and free . . . it expects what never was and never will be." As individuals and as a nation, it is imperative that we consider the opinions of others and examine them with skill and discernment. The Opposing Viewpoints series is intended to help readers achieve this goal.

David L. Bender and Bruno Leone,
Founders

Introduction

> *"The term 'racial profiling' means the practice of a law enforcement agent or agency relying, to any degree, on race, ethnicity, national origin, or religion in selecting which individual to subject to routine or spontaneous investigatory activities or in deciding upon the scope and substance of law enforcement activity following the initial investigatory procedure, except when there is trustworthy information, relevant to the locality and time frame, that links a person of a particular race, ethnicity, national origin, or religion to an identified criminal incident or scheme."*
>
> —*United States Senate,*
> *112th Congress,*
> *End Racial Profiling Act of 2011*

Racial profiling in the United States is as old as the union itself. In the late 1700s, free black people in Virginia had to register with the local courthouse and carry their registration papers at all times, lest they be sold into slavery. Registry papers were the only way to prove one was free, and registration had to be renewed every three years. The rules of the free negro registry were severe and were "a means to restrict the coming and going of Negroes in colonial Virginia and other parts of the South," as described by Anita L. Willis in her 2002 article "The Roots of Racial Profiling" for George Mason University's History News Network website. Virginia's free negro registry formed the basis of registries used in other states. The registry rules tightened to the point that by 1806 free black people were banned from living in Virginia for the next thirty-one years and were only allowed to return because white citizens needed their skills and petitioned for them to be allowed back into the state.

After the American Civil War (1861–65), Virginia's free negro registry was abandoned, but new segregation laws rose in their place by the late 1870s; these were commonly known as Jim Crow laws. These laws, generally applied only in Southern states, segregated white people from black people in public spaces such as schools, churches, restaurants, bathrooms, and public transportation. Jim Crow laws supported the treatment of black people as outcasts within American society. Black individuals were free from slavery, but they were not free to eat at any restaurant or live in any neighborhood of their choosing. Jim Crow laws persisted for almost ninety years, until they were repealed during the civil rights movement of the 1960s. Segregation in Northern states was supported more by tradition and expectation (*de facto*) rather than by law (*de jure*).

Legal equality for people of color has improved since the 1960s, although attitudes have been slower to overcome. Some whites still automatically perceive people with a darker skin color as foreign, unwanted, dishonest, incapable, violent, or immoral. These subtle, and sometimes unsubtle, attitudes feed discriminatory behavior, including discriminatory racial profiling. Following the 2009 arrest of Harvard professor Henry Louis Gates Jr.—a black man—Richard Fausset and P.J. Huffstutter published an article in the *Los Angeles Times* in which they discussed with other successful black men the reality of profiling in the early twenty-first century. These men shared their stories of what they believe is discriminatory racial profiling. Kwame Dunston, a school administrator, said he has been pulled over twenty times in ten years but has rarely been ticketed. Tony Spearman-Leach, former chief of communications at the Charles H. Wright Museum of African American

15

History in Detroit, said he is pulled over about once per year. Like Dunston, Spearman-Leach reported that he is calm, respectful, and cooperative, and does not seek to challenge the status quo of racial profiling as Gates did. Lawrence Otis Graham, a writer, said that affluent black people experience even more profiling because they often live in upscale neighborhoods and dine at expensive restaurants, both places where they stand out and where people assume they are either burglars or staff. Even with a black president in office, Fausset and Huffstutter conclude, taking a stand for one's constitutional rights has limited positive returns for profiled minorities.

Although racial profiling has long been linked with black men and more recently with Arab Muslims, it is not inherently about people of color. Racial profiling can also apply to white people if the known suspect is white; however, these are not the criminal cases that get widely reported. In *Opposing Viewpoints: Racial Profiling*, the contributors examine the various aspects of and controversies surrounding racial profiling. Authors debate the relevance of racial profiling in contemporary society in the following chapters: Does Racial Profiling Exist?, Should Arab Muslims Be Profiled in the War on Terror?, Is Racial Profiling Justifiable?, and What Are the Consequences of Racial Profiling?

CHAPTER 1

Does Racial Profiling Exist?

Chapter Preface

Many minority groups claim that racial profiling is still a reality of daily life in the United States. Some feel they are profiled by police for the color of their skin, while others feel they are profiled at airport security for their manner of dress or for having an Arabic name. Still more assert, as Heather Mac Donald did in her seminal 2001 article for *City Journal*, that racial profiling is a myth, born out of a misunderstanding about how empirical evidence is collected and interpreted. Racial profiling can be difficult to debate, given the strong emotions with which it is associated, but the use of profiling as a police tool has necessitated a discussion of its merits and shortcomings.

New York City's stop-and-frisk policy, which was put in place under Mayor Michael Bloomberg shortly after he took office in 2002, permits law enforcement to search—or frisk—anyone they stop for questioning and has long been considered by citizens to be a new way to racially profile people of color in New York City (NYC). Since this policy has been in place, stops by police have risen 600 percent, according to a February 2012 news report by *Guardian* writer Ryan Devereaux. African Americans and Latinos made up 87 percent of those stopped in 2011, prompting the New York Civil Liberties Union (NYCLU) to decry the city's stop-and-frisk policy as a form of discriminatory racial profiling and thereby file a federal lawsuit. NYC Police Commissioner Raymond Kelly and the New York City Police Department (NYPD) stand by this policy as a way of reducing crime, citing fewer murders since Bloomberg took office, according to Devereaux.

In May 2012, a federal judge granted class-action status to the NYCLU's lawsuit, according to the Center for Constitutional Rights. Mayor Bloomberg and Commissioner Kelly continue to defend the policy, but in light of the lawsuit, they now support changing how stop-and-frisk practices are carried out to ensure that no one's civil rights are violated. This issue is complicated by the fact that Bloomberg and Kelly have reduced crime in New York City over a ten-year period—whether or not that can be attributed to the stop-and-frisk policy remains to be proven. According to crime statistics from the NYC government website, in 2002 the number of the seven major felonies (murder, rape, robbery, felony assault, burglary, grand larceny, and grand larceny of a motor vehicle) committed in the city was 154,809; this number fell by more than 30 percent to 106,669 in 2011. In 2002 the number of other major felonies (possession of stolen property, forgery/fraud/identity theft, arson, felony sex crimes, felony drug crimes, felony weapon crimes, criminal mischief, and other) was 70,993. In 2011 that number had fallen to 57,240, a decrease of nearly 20 percent. Bloomberg and Kelly argue that they are doing something right, and that racial profiling does not play a part in how NYPD cops conduct their work.

George L. Kelling, writing for *City Journal* in 2009, maintained that cooperative efforts by different agencies to clean up minor offenses and disorderly behavior had a long-lasting impact on New York City, contributing to a steep decline in crime during the 1990s. Kelling and his colleague James Q. Wilson predicted this decrease in their article "Broken Windows," published in the *Atlantic* in 1982. They proposed that cleaning up decaying neighborhoods and punishing minor offenses would go a long way toward quelling larger crimes. Their "Broken Windows" theory was considered racist and a way of criminalizing the poor, who are often minorities, especially in urban centers like New York City. Even though agencies did clean up NYC neighborhoods, any decline in crime was attributed to changing patterns of criminal behavior and the improved economy of the 1990s, Kelling wrote in 2009. In a 2008 article, Kelling reported that a peer-reviewed study by Kees Keizer, published in *Science*, tested the "Broken Windows" theory and found Kelling and Wilson's prediction to be true. It was further proven by similar work done by Harvard University researcher Anthony A. Braga.

The existence of racial profiling is still a matter of debate. Across the nation, people who work in the fields of justice and security do their best to keep communities safe without compromising the civil rights of those who are stopped for questioning. Even universities and employers struggle with the fine line between racial profiling and affirmative action. The authors of the following viewpoints debate the prevalence of racial profiling in America and around the world.

| *"The refusal to admit that racial profiling exists . . . has done much to torpedo nearly every effort by . . . civil rights and civil liberties groups to get law enforcement and federal agencies . . . to do something about it."*

Racial Profiling Exists

Earl Ofari Hutchinson

Earl Ofari Hutchinson is an author and political analyst who focuses on the African American experience. In the following viewpoint, Hutchinson covers the political implications of a Torrance, California, traffic stop, search, and harassment of a prominent African American minister who he explains bore little resemblance to a man wanted by the Torrance police for robbery and assault. Torrance has a history of complaints and lawsuits concerning racism against blacks and Latinos, Hutchinson reports, and the incident ignited a local protest and a racially charged counterprotest. Hutchinson calls for federally mandated collection and reporting on racial profiling to begin to understand the problems faced by communities like Torrance.

As you read, consider the following questions:

1. As described by Hutchinson, what are the physical differences between Robert Taylor and the suspect for whom Torrance police were searching?

2. According to Hutchinson, what other large American cities have been identified as having problems with racial profiling?

3. How many US states already collect data on unwarranted traffic stops, according to the viewpoint?

The throng of angry whites jeered, catcalled, and spat out borderline racial insults at the small group of mostly black protesters. This wasn't a march against Jim Crow in Montgomery, Birmingham, Jackson, Mississippi, or Cicero. The year wasn't 1963. The charged racial confrontation happened on March 14, 2010, in the self-billed All-American, mostly white Los Angeles suburban bedroom city of Torrance, California. The march was called to protest the unwarranted stop, search and harassment of Robert Taylor, a prominent Los Angeles African-American minister and civic leader by two white Torrance police officers on March 4. Following the stop, there were hundreds of outraged letters, many filled with vile, crude and profane racist potshots at blacks, in local newspapers blasting Taylor and civil rights supporters.

Innocents Are Targeted Based on the Color of Their Skin

The Taylor stop fit the all-too-familiar pattern of many unwarranted stops of black and Latino motorists. Torrance police officials claimed that he and the car he drove allegedly fit the description of a suspect and car involved in a robbery and assault a day earlier. The problem is Taylor is not even remotely close in appearance to the description of the suspect.

The picture circulated was of a short, stocky dark complexioned 30-something black male. Taylor is tall, in his 60s, and light complexioned.

Predictably, as in most racial profiling allegations, Torrance police and city officials hotly denied the profiling charge. They justified it with the stock story that crime is on the rise in the city, but offered no compelling stats to back up that claim. Taylor's stop would have likely ignited the usual finger-pointing, charge swapping, and then faded fast except for one thing. Torrance has been slapped with a Justice Department lawsuit, civil rights lawsuits, court settlements, and hundreds of verbal complaints over the years by black and Latino motorists; shoppers; African-American mail carriers, some in full uniform that work at postal stations in Torrance; and residents such as Taylor who allege they were racially profiled.

Torrance is hardly unique. [In] the past decade, Los Angeles, New York, Chicago, Miami and other big and small cities have repeatedly been called on the carpet for alleged racial profiling. In an address to a joint session of Congress in 2001, then president [George W.] Bush blasted racial profiling, "It's wrong and we will end it in America." It hasn't.

The Government Should Collect Statistics on Racial Profiling

The refusal to admit that racial profiling exists by many public officials and many in law enforcement has done much to torpedo nearly every effort by local and national civil rights and civil liberties groups to get law enforcement and federal agencies not only to admit that racial profiling happens but also to do something about it. The throng of white protesters that harangued the blacks and other supporters who protested the Taylor stop in Torrance was ample proof of that.

A perennial federal bill served up by House Democrat John Conyers to get federal agencies to collect stats and do reports on racial profiling hasn't gotten to first base. A similar

Racial Profiling Is a Reality in New York City

[In 2010] the N.Y.P.D. [New York City Police Department] recorded more than 600,000 stops; 84 percent of those stopped were blacks or Latinos. Police are far more likely to use force when stopping blacks or Latinos than whites. In half the stops, police cite the vague "furtive movements" as the reason for the stop. Maybe black and brown people just look more furtive, whatever that means. These stops are part of a larger, more widespread problem—a racially discriminatory system of stop-and-frisk in the N.Y.P.D.

Nicholas K. Peart,
"Why Is the N.Y.P.D. After Me?,"
New York Times, December 17, 2011.

racial profiling bill met a similar fate in California in 1999. The bill passed by the state legislature mandated that law enforcement agencies compile racial stats on traffic stops. It was promptly vetoed by then Democratic governor Gray Davis.

Despite Davis's veto, nearly 60 California city and county police departments, the California Highway Patrol, and University of California police agencies, either through mandatory federal consent decrees or voluntary [efforts], collect data on unwarranted traffic stops of motorists . . . to determine if there is a racial bent to the stops. Torrance is not one of those cities.

Voluntary Statistics Need More Rigorous Analysis

Nationally, 46 states collect data, either voluntarily or [are] compelled by state law, on unwarranted pedestrian contacts and traffic stops. Most police officials, as in Torrance, loudly contend that good police work is about the business of catching criminals and reducing crime, not about profiling blacks and Latinos. If more black and Latino men are stopped it's not because they're black or Latino, but because they commit more crimes. The other even more problematic tact used to debunk racial profiling is the few statistics that have been compiled on unwarranted stops; in this case, not by police agencies but based on citizen responses. In two surveys, the federal Bureau of Justice Statistics took a hard, long, quantified look at racial profiling using information that it got from citizens. Both times, the agency found that while whites are stopped, searched and arrested far less than blacks or Latinos, there was no hard proof that the stops had anything to do with race.

This has done even more to damp down a public outcry to get police agencies and legislators to admit that racial profiling is a fact on many city streets and highways and then to take firm action to eliminate it.

The arrest last July of Harvard University professor Henry Louis Gate's touched off a brief furor over racial profiling. Taylor's stop and search has done the same in a bedroom Southern California city. It has again cast the ugly glare on the always troubling problem of racial profiling.

> *"Consider: If you were a police officer in downtown Los Angeles, and you were interested in curtailing crime on your beat, on which group would you focus your efforts, the white, yuppie condo dwellers or the black ex-cons?"*

Racial Profiling: The Myth That Never Dies

Jack Dunphy

Jack Dunphy is a police officer with the Los Angeles Police Department (LAPD). In the following viewpoint, Dunphy addresses the findings of a report on racial profiling in Los Angeles sponsored by the American Civil Liberties Union (ACLU) and authored by Ian Ayres and Jonathan Borowsky. Dunphy argues that this report is biased and flawed. Neither peer-reviewed nor published, its findings conveniently dovetail with the politics of the ACLU, and its statistics are distressingly weak, Dunphy points out. Ayres and Borowsky also fail to compare their results against crime statistics based on race and ethnicity, he adds. Looking at US census data, Dunphy finds similarities between crime rates and percentages of the population for many ethnicities but not for blacks, who have a much higher crime rate as compared to population percentage.

As you read, consider the following questions:

1. According to Dunphy, what is the range of reporting time covered by the Ayres and Borowsky report? For how many months was this study conducted?

2. What explanation do Ayres and Borowsky overlook as a reason why more blacks are stopped by the LAPD than live in the patrolled area, according to Dunphy?

3. In 2007 what percentage of the Los Angeles population was black, according to the viewpoint? What percentage of murder victims in LA were black? What is the disparity between these numbers?

More than seven years ago, Heather Mac Donald wrote "The Myth of Racial Profiling" for the Manhattan Institute's quarterly, *City Journal*. "The anti-profiling crusade," Mac Donald wrote, "thrives on an ignorance of policing and a willful blindness to the demographics of crime." This ignorance persists, and last week saw the arrival of yet another shining example of it. But, unlike the bleating from such charlatans as Al Sharpton and Jesse Jackson, this latest bit of ignorance comes cloaked in the legitimizing finery of Ivy League science.

Last Monday, the ACLU of Southern California released a report titled "A Study of Racially Disparate Outcomes in the Los Angeles Police Department," by Ian Ayres, a professor at Yale Law School, and Jonathan Borowsky, formerly a research assistant at Yale Law School and currently a student at Harvard Law School. The study examined data collected during pedestrian and vehicle stops made by LAPD officers from July 2003 to June 2004. "We find prima facie evidence," write Ayres and Borowsky, "that African Americans and Hispanics are over-stopped, over-frisked, over-searched, and over-arrested." Among their more detailed conclusions are these:

Per 10,000 residents, the black stop rate is 3,400 stops higher than the white stop rate, and the Hispanic stop rate is almost 360 stops higher.

Relative to stopped whites, stopped blacks are 127% more likely and stopped Hispanics are 43% more likely to be frisked.

Relative to stopped whites, stopped blacks are 76% more likely and stopped Hispanics are 16% more likely to be searched.

Relative to stopped whites, stopped blacks are 29% more likely and stopped Hispanics are 32% more likely to be arrested.

Damning stuff, says the ACLU, which commissioned the study. In an accompanying letter to the Los Angeles police commission, ACLU staff attorney Peter Bibring writes that "Prof. Ayres's report ends debate about the existence of the problem and validates the experience in communities of color of police interactions attributable to 'driving while black' or 'driving while brown.'"

Rubbish.

First of all, to claim that a study commissioned by an interest group, especially one as driven by ideology as the ACLU, is so irrefutably grounded in fact as to end debate on the matter is the very height of arrogance. Furthermore, the Ayres report has been neither peer-reviewed nor published in any scientific journal. That the report's conclusions reflect the beliefs of the organization that paid for it should come as a surprise to no one. Indeed, the ACLU may have selected Mr. Ayres on the basis of his keen ability to detect racial bias nearly everywhere he looks. He has previously published books and articles on the hidden racial components involved in setting bail, purchasing automobiles, and tipping taxicab drivers.

Also, if the ACLU had truly been intent on ending the debate, they might have chosen a researcher whose résumé is less blemished by controversy. Last October, the *Yale Daily News* reported that Ayres's latest book, *Super Crunchers: Why Thinking-By-Numbers Is the New Way to Be Smart*, contained passages that were "unattributed verbatim reproductions or nearly identical paraphrases of passages from various newspaper and magazine articles published in the last twenty years." Ayres apologized for the "errors," and said his publisher would make the appropriate changes in any future printings of the book.

Putting aside niggling questions of citations and quotation marks in his earlier work, Ayres's report on the LAPD should stand or fall on its own merits. The reader can well imagine what my own opinion on the report might be, but my position as an LAPD officer may invite skepticism as to my objectivity. So I invited a respected academian to read the Ayres report and offer his opinion on its research methods and conclusions.

David Klinger is an associate professor of criminology and criminal justice at the University of Missouri—St. Louis, and the author of *Into the Kill Zone: A Cop's Eye View of Deadly Force*. He is himself a former police officer, having served with the LAPD and the Redmond, Wash., police department. But he is no shill for cops: He has testified as an expert witness both for and against police officers in civil cases arising from use-of-force incidents.

Klinger expressed a number of reservations on the Ayres report, beginning with its reliance on population figures in calculating what it labels as excessive stops, searches, and arrests of blacks and Hispanics in Los Angeles. In an e-mail to me, Klinger wrote that Ayres's use of the racial and/or ethnic composition of a given area as expressed in census data is not sound. The key question is not who lives in a given area, says Klinger, but rather who is actually present in the area and interacting with the police.

For example, the Ayres report identifies two LAPD patrol divisions (out of eighteen) where the "stop rate" for blacks actually exceeded the number of blacks living in those areas. These disparities are easily explained, yet the report makes only a passing effort at doing so. "Residents can be stopped more than once," write Ayres and Borowsky, "and non-residents who travel into a division can also be stopped."

This last point bears further explication which Ayres and Borowsky do not provide. For example, they fail to account for the large number of homeless men living in downtown Los Angeles, where, according to their report, the number of blacks stopped exceeded the number of blacks living in the area. In recent years a large amount of unused office and industrial space in downtown L.A. has been converted into condominiums and lofts, the residents of which are for the most part white and fairly affluent. But the LAPD's Central Division is also home to the city's skid row, whose "residents" sleep outdoors or in homeless shelters and often go uncounted in census tabulations. These homeless men are overwhelmingly black, and their numbers include a large contingent of paroled felons and others with long criminal records. Consider: If you were a police officer in downtown Los Angeles, and you were interested in curtailing crime on your beat, on which group would you focus your efforts, the white, yuppie condo dwellers or the black ex-cons?

The situation is similar in Hollywood Division, where the black population is no more than six or seven percent. Unexamined in the Ayres report is the fact that Hollywood is home to many nightclubs that regularly attract large numbers of black gang members from South Central Los Angeles and elsewhere. These gang members are responsible for a disproportionate amount of the crimes committed in Hollywood, most especially violent crimes, and thus are far more likely to attract the attention of the police.

> ## Police Officers' Actions Are Interpreted as Racist Despite Data Proving Otherwise
>
> Whatever they do, the cops can't win. Blacks don't get stopped more often? Big deal. Blacks have higher arrest rates? Proof of racism. More blacks are let off without a warning? More proof of racism.
>
> *Steve Chapman, "The Racial Profiling Myth Lives On," RealClearPolitics, May 6, 2007. www.realclearpolitics.com.*

The biggest problem with the Ayres report, says Klinger, is that it presents no ethnic- or race-based crime information, i.e., the amount of crime actually committed by blacks and Hispanics. "Ayres admits this is a liability," said Klinger in his e-mail to me, "but downplays it and uses 'indirect benchmarks' (last paragraph of page 27) to try to overcome this problem. I find this practice quite wanting." Klinger went on to say that Ayres and Borowsky were "speaking beyond the data" in that they did not include in their analysis a critical variable that even they admit must be taken into account in order to draw valid conclusions.

Though LAPD Chief William Bratton was critical of the Ayres report, he has as yet failed to disclose the information Klinger found lacking, information that is readily available and would surely refute the report's bottom line, to wit, that blacks in Los Angeles, and to a lesser extent Hispanics, commit crimes at a far greater rate than do whites, and are therefore subjected to a greater level of attention from police officers on patrol. If one accepts the murder rate as a benchmark for measuring violent crime, the racial disparities are indeed striking. In 2007, the LAPD investigated 394 murders. According to the U.S. Census Bureau, the population of Los Angeles is 9.6 percent black, yet of those 394 murder victims, 134, or 34 percent, were black. And of the 354 identified murder suspects, 129 (36 percent) were black. The number of Hispanic murder victims and suspects roughly mirror the overall Hispanic population in Los Angeles. Hispanics make up 49 percent of the city's population, and last year 54 percent of its murder victims and 55 percent of its murder suspects were also Hispanic. (Whites are about 29 percent of L.A.'s population, but in 2007 they made up just 8 percent of its murder victims and 7 percent of its known murder suspects. The nationwide murder figures reflect a similar racial disparity, as revealed here.)

Los Angeles Mayor Antonio Villaraigosa was once president of the L.A. chapter of the ACLU, and the rest of the city government is composed almost entirely of like-minded liberals. They are far too committed to politically correct ideals to disclose the cold and persistent facts that LAPD cops, indeed cops all over the country, know all too well: that the murder statistics cited above are also reflected in every other category of violent crime. Far from being over, the debate over racial profiling will continue for as long as these racial disparities in crime rates do.

| "Profiling on the basis of race, among other characteristics such as behavior, is likely to become a de facto, if not a de jure, policy in our nation's airports in the years to come." |

Affirmative Action Is Racial Profiling

Elvin Lim

Elvin Lim is an associate professor of government at Wesleyan University. In the following viewpoint, Lim compares the reasoning behind arguments for affirmative action and racial profiling, and he demonstrates how they are similar. He assigns liberal political values to those who stand behind affirmative action and conservative political values to those who support racial profiling. He explains that in the case of national security some profiling at airports must occur, but this is for the safety of many, just as affirmative action will help some of these same people, who may be disadvantaged because of their racial backgrounds, get better educations and jobs.

As you read, consider the following questions:

1. How are affirmative action and racial profiling similar, according to Lim? How are they different?

Elvin Lim, "Why Racial Profiling Is Like Affirmative Action," *Out on a Lim* (blog), November 28, 2010. www.elvinlim.com. Copyright © 2010 by Elvin Lim. All rights reserved. Reproduced by permission.

2. According to Lim, what is the term for opposition to racial profiling, no matter how "noble" the reason?

3. What less discriminatory signifiers do opponents of racial profiling suggest be used to identify possible criminals, according to the viewpoint?

The Transportation Security Administration's new video-screening and pat-down procedures have given new fuel to advocates of racial profiling at airports around the nation. Opponents of racial profiling argue that treating an individual differently simply because of his or her race is wrong because discrimination, even for noble intentions, is just plain wrong. Let's call this the principle of formal equality.

Oddly enough, this is exactly what opponents of affirmative action say. They typically argue that some other signifier, for example class, can be a more efficient and less discriminatory way of achieving similar outcomes if affirmative action policies were in place.

This argument is analogous to the one offered by those who are against racial profiling. They suggest that some other signifier, for example behavior, can be a more efficient and less discriminatory way of achieving similar outcomes if racial profiling policies were in place.

It seems, then, that one can either be for race-based profiling *and* affirmative action, or against *both*. What is problematic is if one is for one but not the other. My guess is that most liberals are for race-based affirmative action but against racial profiling, and most conservatives are against race-based affirmative action but for racial profiling. Inconsistency?

How a Pro–Affirmative Action, Anti–Racial Profiling Position Works

The problem is harder to resolve for the conservative who is anti–affirmative action but for racial profiling than it is for the liberal who is pro–affirmative action and anti–racial pro-

Affirmative Action Is Not Better than Racial Profiling

Affirmative action and racial profiling are essentially the same. Affirmative action amounts to the use of race as a proxy for other, harder to discern qualities: racial victimization, poverty, cultural deprivation. Few critics of affirmative action are against compensating victims of specific and proven acts of racial discrimination. . . . What they object to is generalizing these conditions from a person's race.

Michael Brus, "Proxy War,"
Slate, July 9, 1999. www.slate.com.

filing. Here is why. The liberal can restate his or her philosophy as such: Discrimination is wrong only when a historically disadvantaged group bears the brunt of a particular policy (as in racial profiling); discrimination is permissible when historically advantaged groups bear the brunt of a particular policy (as in affirmative action). By moving away from formal equality toward a more substantive conception of equality that incorporates the principle of historical remedy, a liberal can remain consistently pro–affirmative action, and still be anti–racial profiling.

For the conservative who is against race-based affirmative action but for profiling, the problem is stickier. Almost every anti–affirmative action argument I have come across turns on the principle of formal equality: that discrimination on the basis of race is wrong, *no matter what the policy intentions may be.*

Suppose, in an effort to reconcile an anti–affirmative action and a pro-profiling position, one argued that discrimination on the basis of race is wrong, *unless it was done in the name of some higher good*, such as national security.

Profiling at Airports Will Become Acceptable for the Greater Good

Well, then in protest, the pro–affirmative action liberal will simply substitute "some higher good" with "diversity," and the anti–affirmative action conservative would be forced to accept the plausibility of the liberal's position on affirmative action—or at least the fact that they share similar argumentative forms with no way to adjudicate between one higher good and another (while retaining his or her pro-profiling stance). The problem is that to admit of *any* higher principle other than formal equality (the claim that discrimination on the basis of race for any reason is just flat out wrong) to help distinguish the cases decimates the case against affirmative action that was itself built on formal equality.

Profiling on the basis of race, among other characteristics such as behavior, is likely to become a de facto [in effect, though not formally recognized], if not a de jure [based on law], policy in our nation's airports in the years to come. It is going to inconvenience some innocent people simply because, among other factors, their skin was colored a particular way just as, and the hope is, it will save a lot more innocent people a lot of hassle if everyone were treated equally at airports. If Americans accept this trade-off to be worth it, then perhaps we should also accept the analogous trade-off: that as affirmative action on the basis of race, among other characteristics such as gender, has become law and policy in employment and college admissions, the policy is going to make things harder for some equally qualified people, but it is going to make things easier for a bunch of people who would otherwise have had to endure many obstacles to employment and admission to college.

> "Affirmative action does not seek to create a system of unearned black and brown advantage, but merely to shrink unearned white advantage."

Affirmative Action Is Not Racial Profiling

Tim Wise

Tim Wise is an author, public speaker, and antiracism trainer who has helped numerous corporations and government agencies dismantle institutional racism. In the following viewpoint, Wise addresses the common question of how affirmative action is different from traditional, racist discrimination. He examines the intent, function, impact, and outcome of affirmative action and traditional discrimination, drawing distinctions between advantages offered to whites through discrimination and attempting to level the field through affirmative action. Despite affirmative action, statistics show that whites still are advantaged in educational opportunities and employment; proof, Wise argues, not that whites are more superior but that the work of affirmative action still has a long way to go as the roots of traditional discrimination run deep.

As you read, consider the following questions:

1. According to Wise, how does the intent of discrimination differ from the intent of affirmative action?

2. According to Wise, does affirmative action deprive white people of equal consideration for enrollment at universities, employment, and other opportunities?

3. Despite affirmative action, what percentage of white people hold management positions in the private sector, according to the viewpoint?

Although discrimination against people of color and affirmative action both involve race-based considerations, historic and contemporary discrimination against people of color differs from affirmative action in a number of distinct ways, both in terms of intent and the underlying premises of each, and in terms of the impact or consequences of each.

In terms of intent, affirmative action is nothing like old-fashioned or ongoing discrimination against people of color. Discrimination against so-called racial minorities has always been predicated on the belief that whites were more capable than people of color in terms of their abilities, and more deserving of consideration with regard to their rights and place in the nation. So when employers have refused to hire blacks, or have limited them to lower-level positions, this they have done because they view them as being less capable or deserving than whites—as less desirable employees. Likewise, racial profiling is based on pejorative assumptions about black and brown criminality and character. Housing discrimination is rooted in assumptions about folks of color being less desirable as neighbors or tenants.

Affirmative Action Corrects Problems of Equality Within the Social Order

Affirmative action, on the other hand, does not presume in the reverse that whites are inferior to people of color, or less desirable as workers, students or contractors. In fact, it presumes nothing at all about white abilities, relative to people of color. It merely presumes that whites have been afforded *more-than-equal, extra* opportunity relative to people of color, and that this arrangement has skewed the opportunity structure for jobs, college slots and contracts. Affirmative action is not predicated on any assumptions about whites, *as whites*, in terms of our humanity, decency, intelligence or abilities. It is based solely on assumptions about what being white has meant in the larger social structure. It casts judgment upon the social order and its results, not people per se. Although one is free to disagree with the sociological judgment being rendered in this case—that the social structure has produced disparities that require a response—it is intellectually dishonest and vulgar to compare this presumption about the social structure to the presumption that black people are biologically, culturally or behaviorally inferior to whites.

Additionally, discrimination against people of color has always had the intent of creating and protecting a system of inequality, and maintaining unearned white advantage. Affirmative action does not seek to create a system of unearned black and brown advantage, but merely to shrink unearned white advantage. In other words, unless one presumes there is no difference between policies that maximize inequality and those that seek to minimize it, it is impossible to compare affirmative action to discrimination against people of color, in the past or present.

Affirmative Action vs. Old-School Discrimination: Differences in Impact and Outcome

In terms of impact, affirmative action and discrimination against people of color are completely different. Discrimination against people of color, historically and today, deprives those people of color of the right to equal consideration for various opportunities on equitable terms. While some may think affirmative action does the same thing to whites, in fact this is untrue. Affirmative action programs only deprive whites, in effect, of the ability to continue banking our *extra* consideration, and the credentials and advantages we have accumulated under a system of unfairness, which afforded us *more-than-equal* opportunities. There is no moral entitlement to the use of such advantages, since they have not come about in a free and fair competition. History—and ongoing racial bias against people of color—have served as "thumbs on the scale" for whites, so to speak. Or even more so, as the equivalent of a "Warp Speed" button on a video game. Merely removing one's finger from the warp speed button cannot address the head start accumulated over many generations, nor the mentality that developed as a justification for that head start: a mentality that has sought to rationalize and legitimize the resulting inequities passed down through the generations. So affirmative action is tantamount to hitting a warp speed button for people of color, in an attempt to even out those unearned head starts, and allow everyone to compete on as level a playing field as possible. To not do so would be to cement the head start that has been obtained by whites, and especially white men, in the economic and educational realms. It would be like having an 8-lap relay race, in which one runner has had a 5-lap head start, and instead of placing the second runner at the same point as the first, so as to see who really is faster, we were to merely proclaim the race fair and implore the runner who had been held back to "run faster" and try harder, fairness be damned.

The Slight Impact of Affirmative Action

Finally, discrimination against people of color, historically, has had the real social impact of creating profound imbalances, inequities and disparities in life chances between whites and people of color. In other words, the consequences of that history have been visible: It has led to wealth gaps of more than 10:1 between whites and blacks, for instance (and 8:1 between whites and Latinos). It has led to major disparities in occupational status, educational attainment, poverty rates, earnings ratios, and rates of home ownership. Affirmative action has barely made a dent in these structural inequities, in large part because the programs and policies have been so weakly enforced, scattershot, and pared back over the past twenty years. So despite affirmative action, whites continue (as I document in my books, *Colorblind* and *Affirmative Action: Racial Preference in Black and White*) to receive over 90 percent of government contracts, to hold over 90 percent of tenured faculty positions, to hold over 85 percent of management-level jobs in the private sector workforce, to be half as likely as blacks to be unemployed (even when only comparing whites and blacks with college degrees), and to get into their college of first choice at higher rates than African Americans or Latinos.

In other words, when institutional racism is operating, we can actually *see the results*. We can see the aftereffects in terms of social disparities that favor the group receiving all the preferences. But affirmative action has produced no such disparities, in reverse. It hasn't even really closed the existing ones all that much. So if anything, a proper critique of affirmative action would insist that it hasn't gone far *enough*, or been enforced enough to break the grip of white institutional privilege.

The Racist Underpinning of Anti–Affirmative Action Sentiment

Although not all who oppose affirmative action are racists who purposely seek to maintain institutionalized white advantage, the underlying premise of the anti–affirmative action position comes dangerously close to being intrinsically racist in nature. After all, affirmative action rests on the premise that, in the absence of institutional obstacles to equal opportunity—both past and present—people of color would have obtained positions across the occupational structure, and throughout academia and business, roughly equal to their percentages of the national population. So, on this view, affirmative action merely seeks to create a distribution of jobs, college enrollments and contract opportunities more similar to that which would have been obtained anyway in a just society. To reject this premise is to believe, virtually by definition, that people of color are inferior, and that they would have lagged significantly behind whites anyway, even if equal opportunity had ruled the day. Either because of biological or cultural inadequacy, black and brown folks would simply have failed to obtain a much better outcome than they did under conditions of formal apartheid and oppression. Therefore, to this way of thinking, affirmative action artificially elevates those who would have failed if left to their own devices—at least, relative to whites—and injures whites who naturally would have ended up on top, and who because of their merits deserve to do so.

Despite the fact that this is simply absurd—and the research here is clear, indicating that contract dollars flow to old boy's networks largely unrelated to objective merit—on a purely philosophical and analytical level as well, this argument is nonsensical.

Fact is, even were we to accept the fundamentally racist notion that whites as a group really are superior in terms of ability, intelligence, drive and determination relative to blacks and other people of color, and thus, that even in a system without artificial impediments, those people of color would lag behind whites in all areas of human well-being, the fact would remain, there *were* such impediments, and many of these remain in place today. And those impediments matter, above and beyond whatever "natural" inequities the racist mind might envision existing anyway. And those additional disparities require our attention, no matter what one may think about the inherent inequities between so-called racial groups.

The Tennis Analogy
of Racist Discrimination

By way of analogy, consider the following: Imagine that tennis stars, Rafael Nadal and Andy Roddick were to play 100 matches: roughly two a week, for the next year. Statistically, Nadal is the stronger player. He is, simply, better than Roddick. But yet, the better player doesn't always win every competition, despite their advantage. So we might expect, rather than winning every time, that Nadal would emerge victorious, say, 70 times. But imagine now that we were to place ankle weights on Roddick, or prohibit him, by rule, from using backhand strokes, thereby forcing him to run around every Nadal ground stroke to his backhand court. Needless to say, given such artificial limitations, Roddick would now lose nearly every time, certainly more often than nine in ten matches. The fact that Nadal would have won most of the time anyway says nothing about how unfair the artificial impediments placed upon Roddick would be in this instance. And had those impediments not been there, the results, though uneven, would not have been nearly as lopsided as they were. Surely, even someone who starts from the racist assumption that whites would have naturally beaten out people of color for most of the best jobs, contracts and college slots, cannot help but admit that if "only" nature had been operating— rather than nature *plus* artificially imposed obstacles for people of color and artificial boosts for whites—whatever gaps emerged would, by necessity, be smaller than the ones we see now.

Affirmative Action Is Necessary to Balance
Out Racist Discrimination

So in order to create a just society, in which people can prove themselves on their merits, we must have as close to an equal footing for all as possible. Even if the racists were right—and they are not—that some groups are simply "better" than others, there would be no way to tell which of the individuals in those various groups were the superior or inferior ones, unless all are afforded the chance to prove themselves, without the artificial burdens imposed by the society. If affirmative action were eliminated, we would not have the equal and fair race. We would have institutionalized white advantage, unchecked by a countervailing force.

In the end, we really shouldn't think of affirmative action as a matter of racial preference, so much as a preference based on a recognition of what race *means*, and what racism has meant in American life. It is a preference that takes into consideration the simple and indisputable fact that people of color have not been afforded truly equal opportunity. Whereas old-school discrimination against people of color was (and is) predicated on actual value judgments about the ability, character, and value of black and brown folks, affirmative action is predicated on no personal or group-based judgments whatsoever, but rather, upon the judgment that the social structure has produced inequities that require our attention and redress.

We can deal with that reality or not. But for those who would rather not, at least know that *this* is where the rest of us are coming from. Calling affirmative action a form of institutional racism doesn't make it so. And analogizing it to racial profiling—this time of white people—is historically and philosophically perverse.

> *"The Stand Your Ground law, combined with the existence of racial profiling, was a recipe for mayhem that was capable of causing legal homicide against people of color."*

"Stand Your Ground" Laws Legalize Vigilante Racial Profiling

William Covington

William Covington is a contributor to Our Weekly. *In the following viewpoint, Covington discusses the controversial "stand your ground" law in Florida, which, he argues, permits racial discrimination in a deadly form. The lethal shooting of Trayvon Martin by George Zimmerman brought this state law under federal scrutiny, Covington reports. Many have used this law as a self-defense argument since it was passed in 2005, according to Covington. The real problem with this law, he writes, is that the definition of fear varies from one person to the next; he details the 1984 New York City subway vigilante shooting in which the shooter was acquitted as an example of the fear defense. Covington argues that advocates of the law, like Florida legislator Den-*

nis K. Baxley, have reacted to the public outcry by asserting that the stand your ground law does not apply in the Martin-Zimmerman case.

As you read, consider the following questions:

1. According to the viewpoint, under Florida's stand your ground law, in what circumstances is justifiable force allowed?

2. What groups are using Florida's stand your ground law as a self-defense argument, according to Covington?

3. Of what 1984 case in New York City is the Martin-Zimmerman shooting reminiscent, according to Covington?

Ordinarily, Feb. 26, 2012, would have been a normal day for Patricia A. Wallace, a noted Michigan-based clinical psychologist. She had left her practice and was driving home with her radio tuned as usual to the Rev. Al Sharpton show.

But as she listened, Wallace realized that the legislative monster she had fought against since before its adoption in 2005 was being discussed on the air—an African American Florida youth had been killed and the killer was using as a shield the notorious Stand Your Ground law.

Florida Passes the Stand Your Ground Law

Florida was the first state to adopt the law that governs residents' use of deadly force as a defense. Gov. Jeb Bush signed Senate Bill 436 into law in April 2005, which expands and clarifies Floridians' self-defense rights against violent attackers.

The law allows the justifiable use of force in home protection, or when there is a presumption of death or great bodily harm, or "if a person is presumed to have held a reasonable fear of imminent peril of death or great bodily harm to himself or herself, . . . if the person against whom the defensive force was used was in the process of unlawfully and forcefully entering, or had unlawfully and forcibly entered a dwelling, residence, or occupied vehicle, or if that person had removed or was attempting to remove another against that person's will from the dwelling, residence, or occupied vehicle" and "the person who uses defensive force knew or had reason to believe that an unlawful and forcible entry or unlawful and forcible act was occurring or had occurred."

At least 24 states have adopted some form of Stand Your Ground laws. This week [in May 2012] a task force is meeting in Florida to evaluate that state's law.

Wallace, a mental health professional and college professor with 34 years of clinical experience, was horrified at the news of the Trayvon Martin killing. It was the culmination of the legislative nightmare she had envisioned since the law's inception, and she had written many abstracts about what she saw as its shortcomings.

Trayvon Martin Is Killed by George Zimmerman

By now the name Trayvon Martin is known all over the world. And to some extent, so is the name of his killer, George Zimmerman.

Seventeen-year-old Martin had been watching a basketball game at a friend's apartment in Sanford, Fla. (he was visiting his father). During a break, he walked to a nearby store for candy and iced tea. Upon his return, 28-year-old self-appointed neighborhood watch captain, Zimmerman, began following the youth and reported to a 911 operator that the young man was acting suspiciously. (Much of Zimmerman's conversation with the 911 operator can be heard on tape.) The operator asked Zimmerman if he was following the youth. Zimmerman said yes, and the operator cautioned him not to do that since police were on the way. However, Zimmerman

© 2012 Jeff Parker, Florida Today and the Fort Myers News-Press, and Politicalcartoons .com.

persisted. There was an apparent confrontation during which someone could be heard calling for help. During the confrontation, Zimmerman shot and killed Martin.

Police didn't initially arrest Zimmerman, which inflamed the situation surrounding the shooting. Supporters of Martin's family rallied around and that support has spawned a national movement.

The Stand Your Ground Law Is Ethically Flawed

Wallace remembers arguing intensely to anyone who would listen that the Stand Your Ground law, combined with the existence of racial profiling, was a recipe for mayhem that was capable of causing legal homicide against people of color. Using such a law, an individual could easily kill someone and, with a decent attorney, get away with it. She pointed out that a Stand Your Ground law would further polarize the nation and expose flaws in the law in reference to simple cultural ethnic differences like body gestures, attire, response to questioning by an armed individual.

Already, Wallace stated, more killings of African Americans have been ruled justifiable homicides than the killings of members of any other ethnic group in the nation. However, most of these homicides are a result of black-on-black crime. Oddly, the law has been turned on its ear. Drug dealers and gang members often use the law to escape prosecution from murder on the basis of self-defense.

"This [law] is being used in many, many cases," Florida state senator Chris Smith told the *Miami Herald*. "This is being used with a prostitute killing her john, this is being used in gang fights, this is being used everywhere."

Wallace contended that the law would aid powerful right-wing lobbies like the National Rifle Association.

She discussed the problem of fear.

Variables of the Law Invite Misuse

Fear is generally described as a basic emotion occurring in response to an arousal or sensation that invokes a unique response within each individual. Fear of certain people or situations can be learned and is easily explained by theories of conditioning. The level or degree of fear an individual perceives is dependent on his or her personal history and the circuitry of the brain. Personal fear ranges in degrees from mild caution to extreme phobias that could cause disassociation reaction. Wallace's concerns were that the array of ways that a claim of reasonable fear could be interpreted and processed provides extraordinary opportunities for misinterpretation.

Wallace believes that advocates of the Stand Your Ground laws would likely view standardization of the concept of reasonable fear favorably. They would realize that by employing a standard delineation, the possibilities of misuse of the genuine intent of the law are lessened tremendously.

Jody David Armour, Ph.D., a USC [University of Southern California] law school professor, was asked his views on the law. "When one looks at self-defense laws you would think typically that you can only use legal force to avert a lethal attack, but there are stipulatory principles built into the self-defense law in different states," he said. "Florida is one of them.

"That allows you to use the self-defense law even when your life isn't in danger, just to stand your ground. So it's not only when your life is in danger, but also when you think that you're threatened . . . ," he said. "This is a bombshell when you take into account how black males are seen as a threat throughout the nation by whites. Whether it's a learned behavior from media or culture, the self-defense law could lead to open season on African American males, whose presence may intimidate others."

The Fear Defense at Work

What if Trayvon Martin had a gun when he came in contact with Zimmerman?, Armour was asked. Would Zimmerman have had to retreat or could he have exercised his legal right to stand his ground and defend himself, creating a situation that could have led to a shoot-out?

Armour said that might be the case, but he brought up the 1984 celebrated subway vigilante shooting in New York that involved Bernhard Goetz.

Goetz unloaded on four black youth and a jury acquitted him, even though the youths were running away from him at the time he shot them. The jury concluded that a reasonable person would have been fearful of the youths. So the only question, according to Armour, is whether the jury sympathizes with Zimmerman. If they feel sympathy and empathy for him, they will acquit.

When asked if race will be used by the defense in some form, Armour responded with "No question!" Since Trayvon was black, he [Zimmerman] had a reasonable expectation that he may do him harm. Zimmerman will not say that explicitly, Armour said, but he will subtly get that fear in.

"He will tell the jury look at the person (Trayvon) who was approaching me. 'Look at the hoodie over his head. Where have you seen hoodies like that before? In grainy security camera videos where people are holding up stores.' So an ordinary person (a reasonable person) in my situation would have feared for his life, when he looked at this black young person. You consider gender, you consider age, you consider race. Someone in a Brooks Brothers suit you're going to treat them differently than someone in a hoodie."

The Bernhard Goetz Case

What signal does this incident send to black youth in states that have Stand Your Ground laws?, Armour was asked. "It sends the signal that you should conduct yourself in a timorous and withdrawn fashion whenever you are around anyone who may take you for a threat," said Armour.

Goetz's actions on December 22, 1984, polarized America in a way similar to [the way] the Trayvon Martin shooting has. The Goetz shooting occurred on a subway in Manhattan and it sparked a nationwide debate on race and crime in major cities, and the legal limits of self-defense.

Goetz fired an unlicensed revolver five times, seriously wounding all four youths. He was dubbed the "Subway Vigilante" by the New York press, and was both praised and vilified in the media and in public opinion.

He surrendered to police nine days after the shooting and was eventually charged with attempted murder, assault, and several firearms offenses. A jury found him not guilty of all charges except an illegal firearms possession charge, for which he served a two-thirds of a year sentence.

Trying to Determine Imminent Threat

Law professor Richard Daniel Klein, in an abstract for the *Journal of Race[, Gender] and Ethnicity* titled "Race and the Doctrine of Self Defense: The Role of Race in Determining the Proper Use of Force to Protect Oneself," used the Bernhard Goetz shooting as a test case for an example of deliberate race-based profiling and a race-based shooting. Klein said a valid and appropriate use of self-defense justifies the use of force against another, even when such force results in death. But the force must have been absolutely necessary in order to protect oneself; it cannot have been used as a form of self-help or a display of vindictiveness to retaliate against an individual who may be standing as a symbol for a group that has treated an individual in negative, hostile ways in the past.

According to Klein, Goetz had been robbed previously by African American teens, which may have impacted his judgment in the subway shootings.

Klein believes one has to determine if the threat to Goetz was truly "imminent."

In cases of battered woman syndrome, it has been found that 20 percent of the cases in which the battered woman killed, there was no direct confrontation occurring at the time of the killing. In fact, eight percent of the time the murdered husband had actually been sleeping. But law reformers and women's advocacy groups attacked the requirement of "imminent threat" as being too restricting for the unique position many women often found themselves in. A repeatedly battered woman may well be one who fears the next attack could occur at any time; there was, so to speak, always the threat of an immediate attack.

In the case of Goetz, the so-called dangerous assailants, upon seeing the gun-wielding Goetz, had turned and run away.

Stand Your Ground and Racial Profiling

Klein feels the high crime rate in New York in the '80s may have prevented the jurors from following the instructions of the judge, and they had focused solely on whether the threats against Goetz were truly imminent or were the shootings by Goetz just a release of long-standing pent-up anger and hostility based in part on race? Were the shootings attempts to retaliate for past abuses that Goetz or his family suffered from blacks? Apparently, they saw the shootings as justified.

Florida legislator Dennis K. Baxley, author of Florida's Stand Your Ground law, has been defending the law on national television since the Martin shooting, contending that "it may not have anything to do with the recent death of Trayvon Martin." After numerous calls to Baxley's office in an attempt to ask if he had taken into consideration the impact racial profiling may have played in determining legitimate fear as opposed to racism, we were able to reach staff member Debbie Dennis.

When questioned about the death of Trayvon Martin, racial profiling and Baxley's bill, she said, "We want people to be safe and vindicated from harm. We think Mr. Zimmerman's actions do not apply to the Floridian Stand Your Ground law. We will make further comments after the Task Force on Citizens Safety [and Protection] has reviewed the incident completely."

| "Confronted with evidence disproving their claims of discrimination, race-baiters always shift the standard of proof to make their case just one step harder to discredit."

There Is No Connection Between "Stand Your Ground" Laws and Racial Profiling

Scott Spiegel

Scott Spiegel is a blogger who writes about sociopolitical topics, including the economy, law enforcement, and national security. In the following viewpoint, Spiegel disputes specific claims made by what he characterizes as the liberal media in the shooting death of seventeen-year-old Trayvon Martin by George Zimmerman. Spiegel argues that this is not a case of racial profiling; Zimmerman himself is half-Hispanic and according to the 911 tape, did not single out Martin because of his race, but because of his behavior. Spiegel also disagrees that Martin was a sweet and innocent boy, pointing to his past suspensions from school, possession of stolen property, and misogynistic comments on Twitter as evidence that Martin was capable of hostility. In con-

Scott Spiegel, "Race-Baiters Batting .000 in Trayvon Case," ScottSpiegel.com, April 25, 2012. Copyright © 2012 by Scott Spiegel. All rights reserved. Reproduced by permission.

clusion, Spiegel decries the tendency of liberals to not take responsibility for their own false accusations, as he claims they are doing in the Martin-Zimmerman case.

As you read, consider the following questions:

1. According to Spiegel, does Florida's stand your ground law apply in Zimmerman's case?

2. According to the viewpoint, what behaviors led to Martin being suspended from school, both in the past and at the time of his shooting?

3. What detail of Martin and Zimmerman's altercation was disputed by the media because of poor photographic evidence, according to Spiegel?

Up till now, the most accurate reporting the mainstream media have done on the Trayvon Martin–George Zimmerman case has been relaying the fact that Martin had Skittles and iced tea on him when he was shot. At the rate they're going, I won't be surprised if it emerges that he was carrying Pop Rocks and Four Loko.

Here is a partial list of the wild, reckless, irresponsible claims the left-leaning media have made in the Martin-Zimmerman case, every one of which has been rendered highly suspect or outright false:

Zimmerman is a white racist who killed Martin because he was black.

Multiple acquaintances of Zimmerman's, including black friends, testified to reporters that Zimmerman—who is half-Hispanic—isn't racist. Zimmerman comes from a multiracial family and, during the period when the shooting took place, was tutoring a black neighbor's two young children and helping raise money for her all-black church.

Maybe Zimmerman wasn't racist, but he racially profiled Martin and told a 911 dispatcher Martin looked suspicious because of his race. Zimmerman also uttered a racial slur.

> ## The Reaction to Trayvon Martin's Death Is Overblown
>
> [George] Zimmerman may or may not be guilty; there may or may not be racial motivations [for his shooting of Trayvon Martin in February 2012]. We do not know yet. In the absence of complete evidence, inflammatory comments and belligerent reactions will not aid the search for justice.
>
> *William J. Bennett,*
> *"Rush to Judgment in Trayvon Martin Case,"*
> *CNN.com, March 30, 2012.*

In an egregious act of journalistic malpractice, an NBC producer chopped up the 911 audiotape to make it seem as though Zimmerman had found Martin suspicious because he was black, when in fact Zimmerman was merely responding to the dispatcher's request to identify Martin's race. As for the slur, forensic experts enhanced the sound quality of the tape to isolate Zimmerman's voice and concluded, not that he had used the archaic term *coon*, but that he was lamenting the cold.

Assumptions About Gun Laws and Trayvon Martin

OK, Zimmerman may not have racially profiled Martin, but he was a trigger-happy vigilante who shot Martin because of the cover provided by Florida's barbaric Stand Your Ground law.

As Walter Olson and others have explained, Florida's Stand Your Ground law is utterly irrelevant in the Zimmerman case. If Zimmerman stalked Martin and shot him in cold blood, then obviously he didn't act in self-defense. If Martin set upon Zimmerman, knocked him to the ground, and started pummeling him, as Zimmerman claims, then Zimmerman couldn't have safely retreated, which is what Stand Your Ground opponents would have potential victims do instead of fighting back. Either way, Stand Your Ground has no bearing on the propriety of Zimmerman's actions.

Well, Martin wouldn't have started a fight with Zimmerman—he was a sweet, innocent kid.

The night he was shot, Martin was serving a suspension for carrying a plastic baggie with traces of marijuana. Previously he had been suspended for tardiness, truancy, and spray painting graffiti on school property. Martin had been reprimanded for possessing an assortment of stolen women's jewelry and a lock-breaking device. His Twitter account revealed an affinity for gangsta culture, a flood of misogynistic tweets describing graphic sexual fantasies, and the suggestion that he had assaulted a school bus driver. Photos of Martin displayed a menacing figure grimacing at the camera with a grill over his lower teeth.

Martin's school suspensions are irrelevant. He may have gotten into a bit of trouble now and then, but clearly Zimmerman was lying about Martin bashing his head into the concrete.

Police on the scene confirmed Zimmerman's injuries and the presence of grass stains on his clothes. When ABC News released a grainy surveillance video taken in the Sanford police station that didn't show obvious wounds on the back of Zimmerman's head, the media jumped all over him and called him a liar. When ABC later released an enhanced video that showed clearer evidence of two gashes on the back of Zimmerman's head, liberals claimed the evidence was inconclusive and that conservatives were playing Columbo [referring to a fictional television detective]. When multiple witnesses attested that Zimmerman had bandages on his head and nose the day after the shooting, skeptics questioned the witnesses' credibility. Finally, last week [in April 2012] ABC released a graphic photograph taken just after the incident showing thick rivulets of blood streaming down the back of Zimmerman's head. Liberals have been silent while trying to figure out how to squirm out of the latest corner they've painted themselves into.

Race-Baiters Will Never Take Responsibility

Confronted with evidence disproving their claims of discrimination, race-baiters always shift the standard of proof to make their case just one step harder to discredit, so that they get a clean slate from their previous raft of false accusations and must meet only their current, self-determined burden of proof. When that standard is refuted, they cry, "Yes, but . . ." and move on to the next unmet standard, claiming that all of the previous standards are irrelevant to their case. The logical end point of this burning platform approach to argumentation is for the left to claim that, okay, the facts don't support their case this time around, but the problem they are decrying is nonetheless legion.

If the sheer volume of circumstantial evidence exonerating Zimmerman accumulates to such a degree that a majority of the population comes around to his side of the story, the left won't ever admit that they were wrong. They won't take responsibility for the multiple retaliatory beatings across the country incited by their inflammatory race-baiting. Just as they did with false rape allegations against the Duke [University] lacrosse players, the flurry of phony noose-hanging and anti-black vandalism incidents on college campuses, the apocryphal rash of black church burnings, the Tawana Brawley case [referring to a case in which a fifteen-year-old black girl falsely accused six white men of rape], and a million other made-up incidents, liberals will simply claim that the charges against Zimmerman were fake but accurate, because they drew national attention to a problem that in fact exists only in their heads.

> *"Non-Jewish, especially Muslim, passengers will get a working-over and have to arrive at the airport three hours earlier than the rest of us."*

Racial Profiling Is an Accepted Practice Outside of the United States

Anshel Pfeffer

Anshel Pfeffer is a journalist with Israel's daily newspaper, Ha-aretz. In the following viewpoint, Pfeffer points out that the big difference between airport security in Israel—where there are few restrictions on what passengers can carry—and in other countries, such as the United States and Great Britain, is racial profiling. Pfeffer discusses how, because of ethnic tensions in the Middle East, Israeli airports openly practice racial profiling against anyone who might be Arab or Muslim, or who does not look Jewish, and this is an accepted practice for the safety of all passengers. According to Pfeffer, racial profiling may be the reason why there has not been a successful attack on Israeli air traffic since 1972.

As you read, consider the following questions:

1. According to Pfeffer, what is the Hebrew term for racial profiling?

2. According to the viewpoint, what change to Israeli airport security would cause ticket prices to increase?

3. How many people were killed in the Lod Airport massacre, according to Pfeffer?

A couple of months ago, I toured the IDF [Israel Defense Forces] Ground Forces Command's substances laboratory, a nondescript cluster of prefabricated huts at the Tel HaShomer army base near Tel Aviv, which serves as Israel's brain trust for every type of explosive used by armies and terrorists in the Middle East.

The lab's commander, Lt. Col. Eran Tuval, a goateed officer-scientist with a mercurial temperament, ran around the courtyard, which was littered with leftover Qassam rockets and ominously labeled packages, setting off combustions with a cigarette lighter.

One fact he tried to impress upon me was the ease with which basic household items can be adapted into deadly devices. For example two bottles of liquid, one of them containing the hair dye hydrogen peroxide, can blow up a commercial airliner.

So why, I asked, are we still allowed to board airplanes at Ben Gurion International Airport with bottles and tubes of liquid brought from home, while in [London] Heathrow [Airport] or JFK [John F. Kennedy International Airport in New York] they confiscate our face cream and toothpaste?

"Oh, that's simple," he answered matter of factly. "We use racial profiling, they don't."

Western Nations Are Leery to Use Racial Profiling

Only after the visit, rereading my notes, I noticed a curious detail in his answer. While the entire interview had been conducted in Hebrew, he had said those two words, "racial profiling," in English.

To Israelis, the practice of picking people out based on racial stereotypes is so self-evident, there isn't even a Hebrew term for it. In the ongoing international debate over airport security, which has followed the failed attempt by Nigerian student Umar Farouk Abdulmutallab to blow up a plane carrying himself and 289 others near Detroit [Michigan], much attention has been paid to the methods used to screen passengers at airports.

And though some security experts and commentators, mainly conservative, have advocated adopting racial profiling, the general consensus in the West is that it is unthinkable to subject passengers with certain shades of pigmentation and names germane to a specific part of the world to more rigorous searches.

Some airlines have employed security companies, often run by Israelis, that use similar methods, but on a national level; few Western democracies are prepared to face the storm of criticism they can expect from liberal opinion makers.

Racial Profiling at Israeli Airports Is Open and Expected

As a substitute, American and other security agencies have decided to pay special attention to citizens of various 'suspect' countries, but they are only a small part of the potential suspects. What about Muslim citizens of other countries who may have been radicalized, like the Fort Hood psychiatrist Nidal Malik Hasan [a US soldier who killed thirteen people in a mass shooting]? Neither the American administration nor its counterparts in other Western countries are willing to contemplate a system in which these citizens will be screened differently from their Christian, Jewish or atheist compatriots. In Israel though, there is no question whatsoever. It all happens quite openly. If you have a Hebrew name and 'look Jewish,' the security screening will be swift and painless. If your name is a bit less obviously Israeli, then there are some other key questions.

In my case, they ask how old I was when my family immigrated to Israel and where I served in the Israel Defense Forces, and after that it's easy sailing.

A friend with a similarly foreign name told me that with her, they just hear the Hebrew names of her children and she's okay.

In the case of Jewish tourists, it's usually enough to supply some reliable details on your aunt living in Haifa. We all know why these questions are being asked and we all bear it with good humor. Let's admit it, there is a general acceptance of the fact that non-Jewish, especially Muslim, passengers will get a working-over and have to arrive at the airport three hours earlier than the rest of us.

Of course, they could subject everyone to these inspections, but that would mean we couldn't progress quickly and smoothly from check-in to duty-free, and of course since it would mean hiring hundreds more security agents, ticket prices would go up.

Israelis Turn a Blind Eye to the Profiling of Innocent Muslims

Many Israelis have no problems with this: Let the Muslims suffer for the sins of their brothers. But those of us who like to think of ourselves as liberal humanists find it too easy to ignore the sight of entire families having their luggage rummaged through in front of the entire terminal while we are waved through.

Israel Openly Discriminates Against Arabs and Muslims

In Israel, they didn't pretend that the thorough and condescending questioning of my identity was random, as I'm always assured in the United States. It was blatantly discriminatory, and as I waved to my Caucasian American friends, who told me before they would wait in solidarity outside of the terminal, I was strangely comforted by the openly racist security policy of the IDF [Israel Defense Forces].

Meher Ahmad, "My Homeland Security Journey,"
Progressive, vol. 76, no. 5, May 2012.

Nor do we ever seem to notice the small enclosure to the right of passport control when we return home, where the less fortunate have to wait for hours while they are being checked out. We are in too much of a rush to get through and grab our luggage off the conveyor belts. While governments and citizens of other democracies are dealing with the question of whether they are prepared to live with the chance that their principles and freedoms could lead to a bomber actually managing to activate their hidden device, in Israel that decision has been made for us long ago.

In airports around the world, passengers may have to accept the fact that boarding a plane will become much more bothersome, as they all have to go through the same lengthy treatment, rather than singling out the potential terrorists according to their religion and ethnicity.

Here we don't have that option; the powers that be have mandated that security and the comfort of the majority must triumph. Every month or so, the Israeli media publishes the case of an Arab-Israeli who missed a flight because of the security checks, and of course all of us have privately heard horror stories of visitors who were put through hell. But the basic premise remains unquestioned and the authorities never apologize. These are simply the procedures ensuring everyone's security, they respond.

Racial Profiling at Israeli Airports Works

Perhaps they are right. Racial profiling seems to work. Since the 1972 Lod Airport massacre, in which 26 people were murdered, there have been no successful attacks on Israeli air traffic and almost all the attempts that did take place were carried out on foreign soil. (In the Entebbe hijacking, the terrorists boarded the plane with their weapons during a stopover in Athens.)

Does that mean that while the rest of the civilized world, to which we aspire to belong, are agonizing over these questions, we are exempt from any form of public debate?

"Humiliating every Howard and Hilda heading off on a package holiday, just to meet some artificial racial quota, doesn't serve to make air travel any safer."

Political Correctness Reduces Racial Profiling at British Airports

Richard Littlejohn

Richard Littlejohn is a newspaper journalist for Britain's Daily Mail *and its online version, MailOnline. In the following viewpoint, Littlejohn decries British airport security for unnecessarily searching white passengers so as to not appear racist. He points to anecdotal evidence that white passengers are stopped more often than Asian ones, or even more than Muslim women wearing burkas. Littlejohn makes a case for racial profiling, arguing that many instances of air-traffic terrorism are carried out by Muslim extremists. As an example of not profiling gone awry, Littlejohn points to the Rochdale sex ring into which young white girls were lured by men of Pakistani and Afghani descent. Littlejohn concludes that British airport security should be sensible rather than politically correct in its approach.*

As you read, consider the following questions:

1. According to Littlejohn, why are "innocent white passengers" searched at British airports when airport security is searching for a black criminal?

2. What does Littlejohn report as the repercussion that customers in British airports face if they fight with the staff?

3. According to the viewpoint, who at the BBC suggested that "light profiling" at airports might be helpful, and what was the repercussion of this statement?

White airline passengers are routinely stopped and searched unnecessarily at Britain's airports just so staff can prove they're not 'racist'.

Even when customs officials have been tipped off about a black drugs mule arriving on a plane from the Caribbean, they deliberately intercept a number of innocent white passengers so they can't be accused of discrimination.

John Vine, chief inspector of the UK Border Agency, says staff try to ensure the right racial 'mix' even though they have no legal right to detain people on such grounds.

This is because they are petrified about being hammered with allegations of racism every time they stop and search someone from an ethnic minority background.

Tell us something we don't know. Airport security operates on the same senseless basis.

We've all watched elderly white passengers being put through the third degree, while young Asian men wearing backpacks waft past unchallenged.

I've seen distressed grey-haired pensioners being patted down intimately and forced to empty all their belongings out of their hand luggage.

Meanwhile, women in full burkas are waved through with a cheery: 'Have a nice flight.'

Now I'm not suggesting these young Asian men were planning to blow up the plane, or that the women in burkas were a security risk.

Like it or not, though, the fact is that potential suicide bombers do tend to come from that particular demographic. And al Qaeda suspects have been known to shield their identities behind a burka.

Humiliating every Howard and Hilda heading off on a package holiday, just to meet some artificial racial quota, doesn't serve to make air travel any safer. It is witless, inconvenient and inefficient.

The authorities know that it causes widespread resentment, which is why airports are plastered with notices giving dire warnings that anyone abusing staff will be arrested immediately and prosecuted.

There's something horribly wrong with any organisation which has to threaten its customers with arrest before they get to the counter.

I have to bite my lip every time I travel by air to stop myself railing against the insanity of it all, otherwise I'd be in handcuffs before I got anywhere near the departure gate.

Don't do it, Rich, it's not worth it.

Passing through Britain's airports is already an ordeal. And now that the CIA claims to have discovered a new al Qaeda metal-free explosive device aimed at bringing down aircraft, it's about to get a whole lot worse. Expect even more stringent security, especially on transatlantic flights.

As someone who travels to the U.S. fairly regularly, I'm acutely aware of the threat posed by terrorists. I was on a Northwest flight into Detroit just two weeks before the so-called underpants bomber tried to bring down another Northwest plane above the same airport in 2009. So I'm glad that the authorities are doing everything possible to prevent more aircraft being blown up or flown into skyscrapers.

I just wish a little more intelligence was applied to the process. When was the last time any plane was hijacked by a 78-year-old granny from Leamington Spa? Precisely.

The nature of the threat makes the case for racial profiling at airports compelling. The security services already do it covertly. Stopping and searching those who plainly pose no danger, simply for the sake of keeping up appearances, is obtuse.

Yet when Jeremy Clarkson suggested recently that a little light profiling of air passengers might not be a bad thing, the twittering lynch mob went knee-jerk berserk and there were bovine calls for him to be sacked from the BBC.

Look, I'm not denying there are still genuine problems with racial discrimination. But we've come a long way and it still isn't possible to have a grown-up debate on the subject.

The news has been dominated this week by the conviction of a gang of Pakistani and Afghan men from Rochdale for grooming and sexually abusing vulnerable white girls.

This criminal exploitation had been a problem in some sections of the Pakistani community in the North of England for years. Sue Reid has performed a sterling service exposing it in this newspaper.

But because of the men's ethnic background, there was a reluctance on the part of the police, the Crown prosecutors and the social services to do anything about it. So these girls were abandoned to their horrible fate. The authorities were all terrified of being accused of racism, even though the judge this week acknowledged that these crimes were motivated by the gang's religious and cultural prejudices.

As a direct result of their upbringing in rural Pakistan, these men repress their own wives and daughters and view white girls as trash—easy meat, to be raped at will. Many in the wider Muslim community acknowledge this undeniable truth and abhor their criminality.

Trevor Phillips, head of the equalities commission, hardly a paid-up member of the BNP, has spoken about the madness of transporting third-world village culture to the heart of our industrial cities.

Yet still the police and others, like the preposterous Keith Vaz MP, are insisting mulishly that there was no racial component to these crimes whatsoever.

If it had been the other way round, with white men targeting Pakistani girls, these same lamebrained fools would be howling 'racism' from the rooftops.

While we are all being urged to 'celebrate diversity', we shouldn't try to kid ourselves that multiculturalism hasn't brought with it some serious downsides—such as homegrown Islamist terrorists and gangs of Pakistani child rapists.

We've all got to rub along in this modern-day melting pot. And that noble ambition isn't served by ignoring genuine prejudice where it exists, from whichever inconvenient quarter, and gormlessly screeching 'racism' where it doesn't.

Disingenuously insisting that Pakistani child rapists aren't motivated at least in part by their own wicked brand of racial and cultural bigotry doesn't do anyone any favours.

And neither does stopping and searching blameless white passengers at Britain's airports, when you are hoping to catch a black drugs mule.

That's not a bold demonstration of anti-racism. It's just plain stupid.

Periodical and Internet Sources Bibliography

The following articles have been selected to supplement the diverse views presented in this chapter.

Julie Ajinkya	"'Stand Your Ground' Law Leads to Trayvon Martin's Death: Legal Deadly Force Outside the Home Meets Racial Profiling," Center for American Progress, March 21, 2012. www.americanprogress.org.
Aref Assaf	"Israel's Bad Example: Racial Profiling Is Un-American," NewJersey.com, December 1, 2010.
Dallas Morning News	"Can Big Airlines Like Love Field's Southwest or Forth Worth's American Airlines Tell You What to Wear On Board?," September 3, 2012.
Alan Duke	"Tyler Perry: 'We Are Still Being Racially Profiled,'" CNN.com, April 2, 2012.
Braden Goyette	"Racial Profiling Is Ineffective and Wrong, So Why Does It Keep Happening?," Campus Progress, October 7, 2010. www.campusprogress.org.
Jeff Jacoby	"The Affirmative-Action Myth," Townhall.com, December 23, 2011.
Scott Johnson	"What Ever Happened to Racial Profiling?," *Power Line*, March 14, 2012. www.powerlineblog.com.
Rush Limbaugh	"Why the Left Dropped the Trayvon Story," RushLimbaugh.com, May 16, 2012.
Michael J. Totten	"Forget the 'Porn Machines': How Israelis Secure Airports," *New York Post*, November 19, 2010.
Walter E. Williams	"Is Racial Profiling Racist?," Townhall.com, August 19, 2009.

CHAPTER 2

Should Arab Muslims Be Profiled in the War on Terror?

Chapter Preface

Since the 1970s, Arabs have been vilified in newspapers and films as violent fanatics, a stereotype that was only underscored by Israeli-Palestinian terrorism in the 1980s, the Gulf War in 1990, and increased strife all over the Middle East and Southwest Asia in the early 2000s. The Saudi terrorists who toppled the World Trade Center towers in New York City on September 11, 2001, were identified as members of the terrorist organization al Qaeda, which helped propel the US invasion of Iraq less than two years later.

Abdul Rahman al-Rashed, general manager of Al-Arabiya news channel, wrote in the newspaper *Asharq Alawsat* in 2004 that "it is a certain fact that not all Muslims are terrorists, but . . . almost all terrorists are Muslims," a sentiment repeated by many far-right politicians and anti-Islamic commentators. In the United States, this belief is underscored by the high-profile cases of terrorism carried out by extremists, including the 1993 and 2001 attacks on the World Trade Center, the 2000 attack on the USS *Cole*, and 2009 Fort Hood shooting.

Charles Kurzman, in a report on Muslim American terrorism for the Triangle Center on Terrorism and Homeland Security, writes that fewer than twenty Muslim Americans per year have been charged with terrorism since 2001, a number that is lower than expected by the Federal Bureau of Investigation (FBI), but also not insignificant. Danios of Loonwatch .com used FBI data to compile statistics on terrorism in the United States, concluding in a 2010 article that between 1980 and 2005 Muslims made up only six percent of terrorists. A similar story plays out in Europe, where most terrorist activity is the work of separatists in France and Spain, and Muslims make up less than one percent of terrorists, according to Europol, as reported in 2010 by Danios. These statistics are at odds with al-Rashed's statement that almost all terrorists are Muslim.

This disparity between perception and reality of Muslim American terrorists has been examined by academics. In a 2006 editorial for the Islamabad, Pakistan, *Weekly Pulse*, writer Ishtiaq Ahmad discusses a study by Arab American academic Suad Joseph. Joseph looked at the representation and racializing of Arab Americans and Muslim Americans in major US media outlets such as the *New York Times* and the *Wall Street Journal*. Joseph found that these newspapers, although striving for fair representation, inadvertently differentiated Arab Americans and Muslim Americans from other Americans, painting the former groups as religious, homogenous, and patriotic to their homelands, places often assumed to be in the Middle East. Joseph, as reported by Ahmad, picks apart these assumptions, pointing out that most Arab Americans are Christian and most Muslim Americans are black, not Arab, among other misconceptions.

Ahmad went on to describe the increasing Islamophobia that plagues European countries, especially Denmark, Germany, Italy, and the Netherlands, where large Muslim populations exist. This fear and hatred of Islam is fed by stereotypes—including those described by Joseph in her study—and can best be dispelled, Ahmad concludes, by educating people about Islam, as well as bringing Muslims and non-Muslims together to put a face on the unknown. In an op-ed piece for *USA Today* in 2010, Tom Krattenmaker points out that anti-Muslim rhetoric often comes from conservatives, who, ideologically, have more in common with Muslims than with the non-Muslim liberals who defend them. Muslims and Christians both value "a strong work ethic, devotion to God and family, [and] conservative views on abortion and sexuality."

The threat of terrorism from Muslim extremists and others is still real in the early twenty-first century; law enforcement and the FBI must be vigilant and work to intercept terrorist plots and stop attacks before they happen. Whether or not the profiling of Arab Muslims is a necessary part of this work has yet to be determined. The authors of the following viewpoints examine the many facets of this discussion.

| "Good profiling considers all relevant factors—age, sex, dress, behavior and, yes, race, religion and ethnicity—without regard for political or social concerns."

Arab Muslims Should Be Profiled in the War on Terror

Selwyn Duke

Selwyn Duke is a regular contributor to the daily online publication American Thinker. *In the following viewpoint, Duke argues that racial profiling is an emotionally charged term, but profiling done correctly is a useful tool for law enforcement. He illustrates his point by discussing the profiling inherent in medical treatment, by which some ethnic groups are more prone to inherit certain diseases or conditions. Because Muslim extremists are known to engage in terrorist activity, Duke writes, they should therefore be subject to more—not less—scrutiny. He also rejects the notion that the modesty of Muslim women should be taken more seriously than that of other people. By not directly naming US enemies—such as Muslim extremists—the US government cannot deal with them effectively and the consequences could be deadly.*

As you read, consider the following questions:

1. According to Duke, what is the difference between good and bad profiling?

2. What examples of acceptable profiling are described by Professor Walter Williams, as quoted by Duke?

3. What other group does Duke describe as placing a premium on modesty, along with Muslims?

With all the bad press the TSA has received recently, we can't be sure if the acronym stands for Transportation Security Administration, Touches Sensitive Areas or Truly Scandalous Attention. But, for sure, its pat downs and sci-fi radiation screeners give many of us another good reason to avoid the increasingly unfriendly skies. Yet while the TSA right now has supplanted the IRS [Internal Revenue Service] as the bureaucracy we most love to hate, its policies are merely part of a long-standing cultural trend: The failure to recognize that the good of the many outweighs the good of the few.

It's the same reason why certain cities, most notably London, are now surveilling their residents with thousands of video cameras. If you're not willing to administer punishment sufficient to deter all the criminally inclined save a few intractable miscreants, some of whom you can catch, the only other solution is to have an all-seeing Big Brother that can catch all. It's much like treating a cancer: If you cannot target just the affected tissue, the only other solution is to treat the whole body.

Because the former is preferable not just in medicine but also law enforcement, behavioral-sciences specialists long ago developed the method called "profiling." Unfortunately, social-engineering specialists soon after discredited the universal application of profiling with a method called propaganda. Consequently, when we want to administer targeted treatment in the effort to thwart terrorism, we're told that it's "racial profiling" and beyond consideration. This is utter nonsense.

Profiling Done Correctly Is Fair

As I have said before, "racial profiling" is much like "assault weapon": It's an emotionally charged term designed to manipulate the public. In reality, there are only two types of profiling: good profiling and bad profiling. What's the difference? Good profiling is a method by which law enforcement can accurately determine the probability that an individual has committed a crime or has criminal intent; bad profiling makes that determination less accurate. Good profiling considers all relevant factors—age, sex, dress, behavior and, yes, race, religion and ethnicity—without regard for political or social concerns. Bad profiling subordinates common sense, criminological science and security to political correctness.

Good profiling is also fair. That is to say, it discriminates on the correct basis: If a group—*any* group—commits an inordinate amount of a given crime, it receives greater scrutiny. Period. Bad profiling is invidiously discriminatory. It says, "Hey, if you're male, you'll be viewed with a jaundiced eye. If you're young, then you, too, will be viewed more suspiciously. Don't like it? Take it up with those in your group who commit crimes!" There is no talk of stamping out "sex profiling" or "age profiling." But when we propose applying the same criteria to higher-crime-incidence groups sheltered by the thought police's umbrella of protection, we hear shouts of "racial profiling!" There then are news stories, Dept. of Injustice investigations and people lose their jobs.

Good Profiling Uses Common Sense

Good profiling is also nothing unusual; it's just the application of common sense within the sphere of law enforcement and something we all do continually. If you cross the street upon seeing a bunch of rough-hewn young men walking your way, you've just engaged in profiling. You've also done so if you cut a wide swath around a leashed dog; after all, he may be a very nice pooch, but, since canines are known to sometimes bite, your action is prudent. And it doesn't mean you're hateful or bent on discriminating against rough young men and dogs but simply that you're in a situation in which the cost of obtaining more information would be too great. Consequently, as Professor Walter Williams wrote, "We can think of profiling in general as a practice where people use an observable or known physical attribute as a proxy or estimator of some other unobservable or unknown attribute." He then goes on to write:

> Let's look at a few profiling examples to see which ones you'd like outlawed. . . . Some racial and ethnic groups have higher incidence and mortality from various diseases than the national average. The rates of death from cardiovascular diseases are about 30 percent higher among black adults than among white adults. Cervical cancer rates are five times higher among Vietnamese women in the U.S. than among white women. Pima Indians of Arizona have the highest known diabetes rates in the world. Prostate cancer is nearly twice as common among black men as white men.

Knowing patient race or ethnicity, what might be considered as racial profiling, can assist medical providers in the delivery of more effective medical services.

Now, should doctors be prosecuted for taking these statistics into consideration when delivering medical care? If not, why would we prosecute law enforcement for considering racial and ethnic factors (along with sex, age and other characteristics) when tackling the moral disease known as criminality?

The Profile of Suicidal Terrorists

This brings us back to our current security concerns. The profile here is very specific, as it's a rare person who will sacrifice

Profiling Is Needed to Protect Airline Passengers from Terrorists

Is there nothing we can do to stop this tyranny of fairness? Some semblance of fairness makes sense—and, needless to say, everyone's bags should be screened, if only because it is possible to put a bomb in someone else's luggage. But the TSA [Transportation Security Administration] has a finite amount of attention: Every moment spent frisking the Mormon Tabernacle Choir subtracts from the scrutiny paid to more likely threats. Who could fail to understand this?

Sam Harris,
"In Defense of Profiling," The Blog: Sam Harris,
April 28, 2012. www.samharris.com/blog.

his life to destroy an airplane. Protestants aren't doing that. Catholics aren't doing it. Nor are Buddhists, Taoists, Zoroastrians or Hare Krishnas. In our age, this is a method of [identifying suicide bombers] who 100 percent of the time are Muslim jihadists and 99 percent of the time are non-white. And only the idiotic—or the suicidal—ignores such correlation.

Now, we all know what kind of suicidal idiocy engenders such blindness: a politically correct brand that panders to the sensitivities of vocal, politically favored minority groups such as Muslims. But what about the sensitivities of millions of Americans who have to tolerate intrusive body scanning and pat downs and watch their children subjected to the same? And the kicker is that when Janet Incompetano (as Mark Steyn calls her [referring to Janet Napolitano, secretary of Homeland Security]) was asked if Muslim women sporting hijabs would have to go through the same full-body pat downs, she equivocated and said, "adjustments will be made where they need to be made" and "With respect to that particular issue, I think there will be more to come." Are you kidding me? Is this *Total Recall* meets *One Flew Over the Cuckoo's Nest*? Muslim women are the demographic *second-most likely to commit Islamic terrorism*. If they aren't subjected to scrutiny, what is the point (besides "security theater")?

American Airport Screening Is Biased

Moreover, why should Muslim's imperative of modesty be respected but not other people's? Not only do devout Catholics place a premium on the quality as well, but millions of other individuals find it very offensive to be exposed in front of strangers and groped. Yet we're told that the very group criminological science dictates should receive *more* scrutiny may receive less due to political correctness. And if this actually happens, it will be yet another example of de facto Sharia law in deference to an alien culture and dhimmitude [referring to Muslim rule governing non-Muslim people] for us infidels.

Of course, I realize that Incompetano's equivocation doesn't necessarily mean a Muslim dispensation is in the offing (although I put nothing past leftists), as she might simply have been overcome by the typical liberal reluctance to express unfashionable truths. But is this an excuse? If she expects Americans to tolerate the indignity of intrusive security screening and basically tells them it's tough luck if they don't like it, she has a duty to be just as firm with the over-coddled Council on American-Islamic Relations (CAIR) and its minions. And to not be so was a slap in the face to you, me and anyone who has ever fought for our freedoms. How dare she.

To cement this point, I'll say that this is not first and foremost about whether a given security measure is or isn't prudent. It's also unrealistic to think that we can have satisfactory security without some inconvenience. The point is that whatever methods are settled upon—screening devices, bomb-sniffing dogs, pat downs, etc.—political correctness must *not* factor into the decision. But it does, and this robs the government of all credibility. And I, for one, do not take its efforts seriously.

"Terrorism Is a Method, Not an Enemy"

The truth is that we don't just have security theater but, sadly, war-on-terrorism theater. We launch foreign military campaigns while leaving our back door to Mexico—through which terrorists and WMDs [weapons of mass destruction] can pass—unsecured. We even announce the charade, by calling the conflict "the war on terror." As Ann Coulter once pointed out, using this euphemism is much like having called the WWII [World War II] conflict with Imperial Japan "the war on sneak attacks." Terrorism is a method, not an enemy—Islamists are the enemy. And if we're too effete to even name names, it's no surprise that we won't identify groups.

What I've expressed here is just common sense, but it will remain uncommon unless we experience a cultural transformation. Until the politically correct must keep their death-cult ideology to themselves for fear of scorn, social ostracism and career destruction—the very tactics they've used to silence others—nothing will change. We will continue to exhibit a lack of seriousness about what is a life-or-death issue, a failing that will lead to an inevitable outcome: a mushroom cloud over an American city. When that happens, it will have been enabled by those who gave us our cultural mushroom cloud, ushering in a cold winter of lies and preventing people from seeing the light. And come that time, I hope we remember to thank them appropriately.

> *"Terrorists are multinational, multiethnic and multireligious. Focusing solely upon a particular race, ethnicity, national origin and religion in deciding who to investigate and detain deflects attention from the actual terrorists."*

Arab Muslims Should Not Be Profiled in the War on Terror

Kamalakar Duvvuru

Kamalakar Duvvuru teaches the New Testament in India and contributes to Dissident Voice. *In the following viewpoint, Duvvuru argues that American airline-security agents are indiscriminately detaining and searching people with Muslim names and who have a darker complexion. The problem, he explains, is that people are being treated like criminals without just cause and this plays into the Islamophobia agenda that some politicians and media personalities advocate. White people like Timothy McVeigh commit acts of terrorism also, Duvvuru points out, and some acts of the US government itself are not free from the label of terrorism.*

As you read, consider the following questions:

1. According to Duvvuru, how many immigrants from Muslim countries were questioned in the fall of 2004, and how many were found to be engaging in suspicious activity?

2. As described in the viewpoint, how many times was American Muslim Zakariya Muhammad Reed detained at the Canadian-US border and for what reason?

3. What is the definition of terrorism that Duvvuru provides, and how does he say it fits actions taken by the US government?

One of the draconian consequences of 9/11 [referring to the September 11, 2001, terrorist attacks on the United States] is racial profiling. Bollywood Muslim actor Shah Rukh Khan became the latest victim of what some call "flying while a Muslim" after he was singled out by US airport authorities allegedly because of his Muslim surname "Khan." "I was really hassled at the American airport because my name is Khan," he said. The other recent Indian victim was former president of India. On April 24, 2009, in a clear violation of protocol, Dr. A.P.J. Abdul Kalam, a Muslim, was frisked by the staff of American airliner Continental Airlines.

Shah Rukh Khan was detained at the Newark airport on August 14, 2009, for about two hours, and released only after the Indian consulate intervened and vouched for him. Later he said that instead of doing a routine finger scan, the immigration authorities kept telling him that his name was "common." He said: "They kept telling me your name is common. . . . And I was too polite to ask 'common to what.'" Ironically, his new film *My Name Is Khan* is on racial profiling, and revolves around a Muslim character, mistaken for a terrorist, and his experiences in a post–9/11 America.

Racial Profiling Is on the Rise in the United States

What happened to Shah Rukh Khan is not an isolated incident. Since September 11, 2001, there has been a widely reported increase in racial profiling at US airports, particularly as it applies to passengers with darker complexion, "foreign sounding names," and/or Middle Eastern or South Asian appearance. They are either forced to disembark or refused entry to a plane or detained. Their skin color, names, language and country of origin attract security personnel. Not because they are all criminals. Their "foreign marks" make them suspects. A 50-page report of Amnesty International, "Threat and Humiliation: Racial Profiling, Domestic Security, and Human Rights in the United States," released on September 13, 2004, asserts that racial profiling in the US is pervasive and law enforcement uses race, religion, country of origin, or ethnic and religious appearance as a proxy for criminal suspicion. "Prior to 9/11, racial profiling was frequently referred to as 'driving while black,'" the report noted. "Now, the practice can be more accurately characterized as driving, flying, walking, worshipping, shopping or staying at home while Black, Brown, Red, Yellow, Muslim or of Middle Eastern appearance."

According to the newly released government data, more than 2000 immigrants from Muslim-majority nations were singled out as possible national security threats and questioned in the fall of 2004. After being questioned about their views on the United States and what was preached in their mosques, none of those interrogated were charged with national security offenses. Of course, security personnel should interrogate individuals who arouse suspicion, but to question only members of one religious or ethnic community is unethical, humiliating and ineffective. It is naïve to imagine that all terrorists are Muslim and of Middle Eastern descent.

Muslims Have Been Under Scrutiny in the United States Since 9/11

In 2007 the Los Angeles Police Department [LAPD] launched an extensive mapping program to identify Muslim enclaves across the city. LAPD Deputy Chief Michael Downing told the *Los Angeles Times*: "We want to know where the Pakistanis, Iranians and Chechens are so we can reach out to those communities." But the mapping program has sparked outrage from some Islamic groups and civil libertarians. The American Civil Liberties Union said that the program was nothing short of racial profiling.

Racial profiling at US airports has intensified after 9/11. On a flight, air marshals and airline crews can force a passenger to leave a plane, or even arrest him/her merely because a fellow passenger or airline personnel feels uncomfortable with his/her presence on the plane. Inevitably, the passengers affected are those with darker skin, and/or Middle Eastern and South Asian appearance. In November 2006 six Muslim imams were led away in handcuffs from a US Airways flight after passengers complained that they were praying in the terminal before boarding the plane. After their release, it is alleged, the airline denied them passage in any of its other flights and also refused to help them get tickets for other airlines. In another incident, in August 2007 at the San Diego airport an American Airlines flight to Chicago was delayed because a passenger was scared of several Arabic-speaking men on board. They were, in fact, Iraqi-Americans, who went to San Diego to train US Marines at Camp Pendleton. The men were detained and questioned before being released. Later the flight was cancelled!

Innocent American Muslims Are Treated with Prejudice

Azhar Usman, a burly American-born Muslim with a heavy black beard, says that he elicits an almost universal reaction when he boards an airplane at any United States airport: conversations stop in mid-sentence and the look in the eyes of his fellow passengers says, "We're all going to die!" Ahmed Ahmed, a comedian who was hauled through the Las Vegas airport in handcuffs, says: "It's a bad time to be named Ahmed now," as his name is a "common" name and could match a member of a terrorist group.

Racial profiling affected those with "foreign marks" at the cross-border also. Zakariya Muhammad Reed, who served for 20 years in the National Guard, and eleven years as a fire-fighter, was detained four times in six months in 2007 at the Canada-US border after he and his family visited his wife's family in Ontario, Canada, and were returning to the US. In the first encounter, he says, the guards engaged in some nasty banter. "You know, we're really too good to these detainees," one of the guards said, according to Reed. "We should treat them like we do in the desert. We should put a bag over their heads and zip tie their hands together." After about three hours, Reed says, they took his photo and fingerprints, and made him wait a half hour longer before giving him his passport back and telling him he could go. "Our car was completely trashed," he says. "My son's portable DVD player was broken, and I have a decorative Koran on the dashboard that was thrown on the floor." Later he was told by Dan Foote, aide to Representative Marcy Kaptur, that the trouble was "no doubt because you probably changed your name to a Muslim name."

Islamophobia Plays on People's Fears

Reed's letter to the Interagency Border Inspection System, sent on February 2, 2007, expresses his agonizing ordeal. "Nobody will give me any information as to why I am being detained," he wrote. "I would like to know exactly what I am being accused of and why is it that I am having so much trouble reentering the home of my birth. . . . My entire life has revolved around the service of American citizens and suddenly I am being treated like a criminal because there 'is a problem with my name,' to quote one of the border officers. . . . What do I have to do to get my name from this list? . . . I have been treated like a criminal and my wife and children have been mistreated and disrespected in the name of Homeland Security. All we want is to go on with our lives as before. I have never taken part in any subversive activity to cause harm to this land or its people. I have never done anything criminal in my life."

The US has been caught up with Islamophobia. This is fuelled by several self-interest groups. Media played its role in stoking up Islamophobia. Radio host Mike Gallagher suggested "Muslim-only" lines for the airports. On November 14, 2006, CNN host Glenn Beck asked the first-ever Muslim congressman Keith Ellison: "I have been nervous about this interview with you, because what I feel like saying is, 'Sir, prove to me that you are not working with our enemies.' I am not accusing you of being an enemy, but that's the way I feel, and I think a lot of Americans will feel that way." Some politicians played their part in supporting racial profiling. After terrorist attacks in London, a New York assemblyman Dov Hikind, a Brooklyn Democrat, said that he would introduce legislation to allow police to zero in on Middle Easterners when they conduct terrorism prevention searches in subways or other local transport systems. In 2008 during the US presidential elections, 28 million copies of a DVD titled *Obsession: Radical Islam's War Against the West* have been distributed within a few weeks in key battleground states. This film features graphic, violent images and makes comparisons of Islam to Nazism.

Islamophobia in the US is clearly reflected by the question of John McCain's supporter: "I got to ask you a question. I do not believe in . . . I can't trust Obama. I have read about him, and he's not . . . he's not . . . he is an Arab. . . ."

White People Also Engage in Terrorism

Not only is racial profiling unfair and unequal, but it also implements a system of racial moral superiority. While it is true that some members of the Muslim community and of Middle Eastern descent were responsible for terrorist attacks in the US, so have "white" men like Timothy McVeigh of the Oklahoma City bombing, and Richard Reid, the British shoe bomber. Adam Gadahn, an al-Qaida spokesperson, is a "white" American from a mixed Jewish and Christian heritage and hails from California. John Walker Lindh, the so-called "American Taliban," is a Roman Catholic. These individuals do not fit the profile used by programs like the National Security Entry-Exit Registration System (NSEERS) and US-VISIT [United States Visitor and Immigrant Status Indicator Technology] that target Arabs, Muslims, and South Asians. Terrorists are multinational, multiethnic and multireligious. Focusing solely upon a particular race, ethnicity, national origin and religion in deciding who to investigate and detain deflects attention from the actual terrorists.

In March 2008, the UN [United Nations] Committee on the Elimination of Racial Discrimination (CERD) issued a strongly worded critique of the United States' record on racial discrimination and urged the government to make sweeping reforms to policies affecting racial and ethnic minorities, women, immigrants and indigenous populations in the US. Among its recommendations, the committee called on the US to pass the federal End Racial Profiling Act or similar legislation and combat widespread ethnic and racial profiling practices by law enforcement, especially against Arabs, Muslims and South Asians in the wake of the 9/11 attacks.

Racial Profiling and the Global War on Terror

Racial profiling in the US has been [known] not only to stoke hatred towards Muslims, but also to fuel the already rampant ethnic and religious scapegoating. The power of "scapegoat mechanism" lies in its deception and concealment. On the one hand, it deceives by depicting those who established "scapegoat mechanism" as righteous and innocent, and the "other" as cause of violence. Thus, it legitimizes all forms of violence (violence as violation of one's human dignity, value and rights) against the "other," and portrays this violence as a "sacred" act. On the other hand, it conceals the innocence and plight of the "other," and the violence of those who scapegoated the "other." It transforms the violence against the "other" as "good violence." Thus, the cycle of scapegoating the weak and vulnerable continues.

Racial profiling has, in a way, secured support of the majority of Americans for the US global war on terror. Moreover, Muslims are perceived by many in the US as "the other," a perception that allows them to be treated inhumanely without mass protest. It is similar to what the US did during World War II to Japanese, leaving out those of German or Italian heritage.

With overwhelming public support the US, along with its allies, launched global war on terror, disguising its real economic and political agenda. Racial profiling . . . perverted the integrity of human conscience, head and heart. It has helped to deflect not only sympathy from the victims of US genocidal violence in Iraq, Afghanistan and elsewhere, but also public focus from "normalized" US human rights violations in those countries. The American public is benumbed to the US atrocities and plunder, incarceration of hundreds of Muslims, destruction of life and property in Iraq and Afghanistan, torture in Guantánamo Bay [a US detention camp in Cuba], Iraq, Afghanistan and other secret prisons, and extraordinary renditions.

US Terrorism on the Muslim World

Robert Fisk said:

> Do we in fact really understand the extent of injustice in the Middle East? When I finished writing my new book, I real-

89

ized how amazed I was that after the past 90 years of injustice, betrayal, slaughter, terror, torture, secret policemen and dictators, how restrained Muslims had been, I realized, towards the West, because I don't think we Westerners care about Muslims. I don't think we care about Muslim Arabs. You only have to look at the reporting of Iraq. Every time an American or British soldier is killed, we know his name, his age, whether he was married, the names of his children. But 500,000–600,000 Iraqis, how many of their names have found their way onto our television programs, our radio shows, our newspapers? They are just numbers, and we don't even know the statistic.

Moreover, the American public has failed to acknowledge that US unlawful use of force against people and property in Iraq and Afghanistan to achieve its political and economic objectives is nothing but terrorism. According to the US joint chiefs of staff publication, terrorism is defined as "the unlawful use or threatened use of force or violence against people or property to coerce or intimidate governments or societies, often to achieve political, religious, or ideological objectives."

The United States Has Engaged in Terrorism

Americans have also ignored US past terrorism history. Pointing out US behavior, in July 2006 Edward Peck, former US ambassador to Iraq and deputy director of [President Ronald] Reagan's task force on terrorism, said:

In 1985, when I was the deputy director of the Reagan White House task force on terrorism, they asked us . . . to come up with a definition of terrorism that could be used throughout the government. We produced about six, and each and every case, they were rejected, because careful reading would indicate that our own country had been involved in some of those activities.

Again in July 2006 Peck said:

U.S. Code Title 18, Section 2331[1], and read the U.S. definition of terrorism. And one of them in here says—one of the terms, "international terrorism," means "activities that," I quote, "appear to be intended to affect the conduct of a government by mass destruction, assassination or kidnapping." . . . Yes, well, certainly, you can think of a number of countries that have been involved in such activities. Ours is one of them.

A concerned Peck in an interview on CNN *Crossfire* on October 8, 2001, retorted, "Why is it that all of these people hate us. It's not because of freedom. . . . They hate us because of things they see us doing to their part of the world that they definitely do not like."

Very rightly Shah Rukh Khan said that America needed to understand that "it's not an isolated parallel universe existence for this country. . . . There is a whole world which makes all the good and bad that is happening. So if you are scared of violence, terrorism, all of us are responsible for it. It is not that the rest of the world is and America is not."

"Can we reasonably expect Americans,
who are themselves collectively targets
of surveillance and suspicion, to trust
the very agencies spying on them?"

Racial Profiling Leads Arab Muslims to Distrust Law Enforcement

Sahar Aziz

Sahar Aziz is an associate law professor at Texas Wesleyan University and a fellow at the Institute for Social Policy and Understanding. In the following viewpoint, Aziz discusses how American Muslims have been lured into relationship-building meetings with federal agencies, only to later learn that they are being spied on. Aziz argues that this behavior destroys crucial trust between the government and American Muslims necessary for counterterrorism information to get to authorities. She also points out that community-oriented American Muslims are not the perpetrators of terrorism; therefore, collecting information on these people wastes time and money in addition to destroying trust.

As you read, consider the following questions:

1. According to Aziz, why are federal bureaucrats really meeting with Muslim leaders in the United States?

2. Who is the primary threat of homegrown terrorism in the United States, according to the viewpoint?

3. According to the author, why would American Muslims avoid reporting suspicious activity?

In the same week, a Moroccan 29-year-old man was caught attempting to bomb the Capitol in a government-led terrorism sting operation and the NYPD [New York City Police Department] was caught systemically spying on Muslim students at Yale, the University of Pennsylvania, Rutgers, and other universities on the US east coast. These two seemingly distinct events epitomize the fundamental flaws in the government's counterterrorism policies.

On the one hand, the government, under both the [George W.] Bush and [Barack] Obama administrations, has expended significant resources to conduct "community outreach" meetings with Muslims across the nation. On the other hand, while Muslims are lured into trusting their government, they are systematically spied on, investigated, and sometimes prosecuted.

Government Agencies Are Spying on Muslim Community Groups

Millions of dollars are spent flying bureaucrats from various federal agencies to meet and greet Muslim leaders, most of whom are male, in an attempt to earn their trust. In those meetings, local and state law enforcement is invited to build long-term relationships with the Muslim communities in their jurisdictions. On the face of it, the meetings appear to be a good-faith effort to demystify Muslims and counter false stereotypes of Muslims as terrorists. In practice, the objectives are more duplicitous.

In a blatant violation of their trust, local and federal agencies are recording these community outreach meetings, as well as the names and personal information of the attendees. Even Muslim imams who have been engaging with the government for years have found themselves under investigation. Community outreach meetings appear nothing more than a tool within a broader fishing expedition of Muslim communities nationwide. The strategy is that if there is no evidence of terrorism, then the government must go out there and create it through community outreach meetings that set the groundwork for sting operations.

In doing so, the government is alienating its most important ally, the Muslim community, which has been the most effective counterterrorism tool the government has.

As witnessed in recent reports of the NYPD's long-term surveillance program, this information gathering is part of a much broader surveillance scheme targeting community leaders, Muslim students, and any other Muslim with the misfortune of interacting with an undercover agent or informant. Without any evidence of criminal activity, informants infiltrated Muslim student organizations at Yale, Rutgers, and other universities. The undercover agents attended student meetings, academic conferences, and participated in field trips. The attendees' names and conversations became the basis of personal files in intelligence databases and subsequent investigations.

Terrorism by Muslims in the United States Is Declining

Meanwhile, the government admits that "lone wolf" terrorists are currently the primary threat of homegrown terrorism in the United States. Despite the conclusions of a recent report by the Triangle Center on Terrorism and Homeland Security that terrorism committed by Muslims in America is declining, the government is focused solely on Muslims. To be sure, reli-

© 2012 Adam Zyglis, The Buffalo News, and Politicalcartoons.com.

gious profiling is the least of the government's concern, especially during an election year when politicians earn political capital by Muslim bashing.

Herein lies the paradox.

Assuming the government's conclusions are correct, lone-wolf terrorists are very difficult to detect because they do not have co-conspirators or networks of support. They are often mentally unstable individuals at the margins of society. To the extent that the lone-wolf terrorists who are Muslim seek to recruit other Muslims, they risk detection. This explains the government's appetite for community engagement in hopes that Muslims will report such interactions.

But can we reasonably expect Americans, who are themselves collectively targets of surveillance and suspicion, to trust the very agencies spying on them? One need only study the experiences of African Americans systematically harassed, investigated, and prosecuted by police. The result is an understandable distrust of law enforcement—so much so that young African American men go out of their way to avoid any contact with the police. Rather than view law enforcement agencies as protectors, they are viewed as persecutors. So long as the police engage in systemic racial profiling and attendant criminal punishments, community outreach is futile, as well as disingenuous.

Disenfranchised American Muslims Are Less Likely to Report Suspicious Activity

Thus, American Muslims face a palpable dilemma. If they report suspicions about terrorism, they invite government scrutiny into their lives and are likely to become targets of informants, investigations, and surveillance (if they are not already). This entails very serious risks to their liberty. If they avoid interacting with law enforcement to protect their civil liberties, however, they are accused of condoning terrorism and disloyalty.

Like any other Americans, American Muslims report terrorism about which they have knowledge. But revelations about the NYPD's surveillance program, coupled with proven surveillance of community outreach meetings, make one thing clear: no good deed goes unpunished for Muslims in America.

"Singling people out on the basis of their race, ethnicity, religion, national origin or perceived citizenship or immigration status is in direct breach of the founding principles of this country."

Muslim Americans Support a Federal Ban on Racial Profiling

Coleen Rowley

Coleen Rowley is a political activist and former Federal Bureau of Investigation (FBI) agent. In the following viewpoint, speaking on behalf of the Muslim Legal Fund of America (MLFA), Rowley argues that the undefined national security loopholes in the 2003 Department of Justice guidance on racial profiling be closed. She points out that American Muslims are being religiously discriminated against, but more data needs to be collected to conclusively prove the ineffectiveness of religious profiling, as has been done with racial profiling. Racial and religious profiling can damage relationships between Muslim communities and police, restricting the flow of information needed by authorities to catch criminals. Rowley and the MLFA call for the passage of the End Racial Profiling Act.

Coleen Rowley, "Statement of Coleen Rowley, Vice President of the Board of Directors, Muslim Legal Fund of America, 'Ending Racial Profiling in America,'" Senate Committee on the Judiciary, Subcommittee on the Constitution, Civil Rights and Human Rights, United States Senate, April 17, 2012.

As you read, consider the following questions:

1. According to Rowley, from what two flaws does the 2003 Department of Justice guidance on racial profiling suffer?

2. Why is research on religious profiling harder to conduct than research on racial profiling, according to the author?

3. According to the viewpoint, what illegal activity targeting Muslims has the FBI allegedly participated in using informants such as Craig Monteilh?

Legal scholars, ethicists and human rights academics had long decried the racial, religious and other kinds of profiling commonly practiced by law enforcement on moral and legal grounds. But it seems the key to success for . . . legal researchers in finally getting many police officials around the country to budge off their calcified reliance upon racial profiling and make a 180 degree turn, about a decade ago, lay in these scholars finally providing solid, statistical proof that profiling simply does not "work." So powerful were their findings, that it undoubtedly was what convinced the [George W.] Bush administration to issue guidance (in June 2003) generally prohibiting all federal law enforcement officers from practicing racial profiling.

The Religious Profiling Loophole Needs to Be Closed

Unfortunately the 2003 Department of Justice (DOJ) "Guidance Regarding the Use of Race by Federal Law Enforcement Agencies" suffered from two major flaws: 1) it applies to police profiling (discrimination) based on race and ethnicity but not to religious discrimination (which is often entwined with ethnicity) even though the guidance, in its first pages, cites the Supreme Court decision in *United States v. Armstrong*, 517

U.S. 456, 464 (1996) for the proposition that "whether to prosecute may not be based on 'an unjustifiable standard such as race, *religion*, or other arbitrary classification'" (emp added) and then adding that "the same is true of (decisions of) Federal law enforcement officers. Federal courts repeatedly have held that any general policy of 'utiliz(ing) impermissible racial classifications in determining whom to stop, detain and search' would violate the equal protection clause"; and 2) the federal anti–racial profiling policy unreasonably carved out a large exemption from its reach for "threats to national security or other catastrophic events (including the performance of duties related to air transportation security) or when protecting the integrity of the nation's borders."

MLFA [Muslim Legal Fund of America] strongly feels there is no good reason for either of these two exclusions; not for the explicit "national security" one nor for the not-so-explicit but merely unmentioned religious profiling one. In fact the failure of the guidance to protect against religious profiling and its failure to generally prohibit racial and ethnic profiling relating to threats of national security and border integrity completely contradict the Bush DOJ's stated rationale for issuing the policy. These "loopholes" should be closed.

Profiling on the Rise in the United States After 9/11

The MLFA has absolutely no doubt that if the relevant data could be obtained and analyzed it would reveal that profiling based on religion in the "war on terror" is as equally counterproductive to public safety as profiling based on race, ethnicity or the color of one's skin was shown to be in the "war on drugs." However, actual statistical proof like that published by Professor David Harris and others in the late 1990s seems to be currently lacking vis-à-vis religion-based profiling, the first cousin of racial and ethnic profiling. There are probably a couple main reasons why there is little hard data focused on authorities' actions focused, for instance, on "flying while Muslim" as opposed to "driving while black." For starters, not much more than a decade has transpired since 9/11 [referring to the September 11, 2001, terrorist attacks on the United States]. Media coverage of the terrorist attacks seems to have quickly shattered the emerging American public consensus that racial and ethnic profiling is wrong and should be eliminated. Polls taken after 9/11 showed a majority of Americans in support of profiling of Arabs at airports and of requiring Arabs to carry special identification cards. Consequently, despite public speeches and reassurances by high-ranking agency and administration officials to the contrary, religious and ethnic profiling is believed to have dramatically expanded. One early indication was when Attorney General [John] Ashcroft relaxed the prior AG [attorney general] guidelines to allow FBI [Federal Bureau of Investigation] agents and informants to attend and target mosques without any specific factual suspicion. Another clue could be seen in the government's instituting of new nonimmigrant registration policies that targeted certain Arab, and largely Islamic countries. Arab Americans, and those with Arab appearances, were increasingly singled out for questioning and security checks based on their skin color, clothing, name, or religious beliefs.

The Truth About Post–9/11 Counterterrorism Efforts Is Emerging

Consequently "a poll conducted in May 2002 found that more than three-quarters of Arab Americans felt that there was more profiling of Arab Americans since 9/11, and nearly two-thirds felt very or somewhat worried about the long-term effects of discrimination. Reports by other state advisory committees to the U.S. Commission on Civil Rights confirm the existence of post–9/11 racial and ethnic profiling, as well as a surge in hate violence and discrimination in the United States against people who are or are perceived to be Arab, South

Asian, or Muslim in the months immediately following 9/11." (District of Columbia, Maryland, and Virginia Advisory Committees to the U.S. Commission on Civil Rights, *Civil Rights Concerns in the Metropolitan Washington, D.C., Area in the Aftermath of the September 11, 2001, Tragedies*, June 2003, p. 1; Illinois Advisory Committee to the U.S. Commission on Civil Rights, "Arab and Muslim Civil Rights Issues in the Chicago Metropolitan Area Post-September 11," May 2003, p. 4.)

Unfortunately, counterterrorism reports on all levels tend to be classified and much harder for legal and human rights researchers to access and study than regular criminal reports. It has taken years for investigative reporters and civil liberties groups using Freedom of Information [Act] requests and other tools to uncover the first bits of real truth and official documentation about how the FBI, other federal agencies and big police departments like the NYPD [New York City Police Department] could have so quickly and simplistically based so much of their "counterterrorism" efforts upon ethnic origin and religion. News has emerged, however, detailing collection/retention of information about various Muslim individuals' religious practices, by law enforcement and national security agencies, in cases lacking any specific factual suspicion. The extent of this collection remains unknown.

Religious Profiling Does Not Work

Anecdotal evidence does increasingly surface of the counterproductive nature of such religion-based profiling, for example the recent news of the NYPD's spying on innocent Muslim college students going on a canoe trip. At the same time, whether due to improperly diverted law enforcement resources or other failures, the real terrorists in recent years (like "Times Square bomber" [Faisal] Shahzad, "underwear bomber" [Umar Farouk] Abdulmutallab and the Jordanian suicide bomber who blew up the CIA [Central Intelligence Agency] station in Pakistan to name just a few of the more well-known recent ones) went undetected and unstopped by national security agencies. This anecdotal evidence would need to be empirically bolstered, however, in order to prove that religious profiling functions as counterproductively as racial profiling. The MLFA would definitely support the collection and study of the type of solid, credible statistics similar to what served to prove that racial profiling was not effective.

Any research will be a lot more difficult to conduct as to religious and ethnic profiling than what Professor Harris published also due to the fact that there are fewer visual cues and due to national security actions being less spontaneous and more based on and entwined with what the *Washington Post* describes as "Top Secret" America's massive data ("intelligence") collection and data-mining programs put into place after 9/11. Besides the classified nature of the data, it was relatively easier, by comparison, to study the "hit rates" of drug/weapon confiscations and arrests following police stops and frisks of black drivers, given the more obvious skin color visual cues. While distinctive religious garb exists in some cases and ethnic origin is often accompanied by skin color and physical differences, the distinctions are not as visible as "race" in allowing legal researchers to determine law enforcement motivations and then examine the effectiveness of such racial profiling.

The Department of Justice Allows Damaging Profiling Loopholes

In any event, the DOJ must have had a reason for allowing racial and ethnic profiling to continue in connection with "threats to national security" as opposed to prohibiting racial and ethnic profiling in connection with other crimes. It should be pointed out that nowhere in the policy is a "threat to national security" defined. Espionage and international terrorism are undoubtedly considered "threats to national security" but what about a domestic terrorist incident like the bombing of the Oklahoma [City] federal building or the series of murders caused by mailing weaponized anthrax, (presumably from Ft. Detrick military laboratories)? Could not massive financial frauds or public corruption also threaten national security? Could not the national security exception allowing racial profiling then swallow the rule?

What exacerbates the problem is that ethnic- and religion-based profiling combines in national security cases with the doctrine of "pre-emption," the belief that it's possible to accurately prevent serious crimes and acts of terrorism before they happen. (A desirable but unrealistic utilitarian outcome like this is often used to justify wrongful, ineffective means, the most common one in recent history being the nonsensical notion, now believed by a majority of Americans inclined to believe fictional TV plots, that "torture tactics are justified in order to elicit information to find the ticking time bomb and thus save lives.") It should be noted that the scenarios furnished in the 2003 DOJ anti–racial profiling guidance exemplifying when a race-based description, along with other factors, does not violate the policy all dealt with past or ongoing specific crimes and not an inchoate future threat. Targeting mosques and Muslim organizations to prevent generalized future crimes and thus contain "threats to national security" inherently contrasts with possession of greater factual specificity about a past crime or reports from an established reliable source about an ongoing crime.

Federal Protection Against Profiling Is Inconsistent

The 2003 guidance states that:

"the President has made clear his concern that racial profiling is morally wrong and inconsistent with our core values and principles of fairness and justice. Even if there were overall statistical evidence of differential rates of commission of certain offenses among particular races, the affirmative use of such generalized notions by federal law enforcement officers in routine, spontaneous law enforcement activities is tantamount to stereotyping. It casts a pall of suspicion over every member of certain racial and ethnic groups without regard to the specific circumstances of a particular investigation or crime, and it offends the dignity of the individual improperly targeted. Whatever the motivation, it is patently unacceptable and thus prohibited under this guidance for federal law enforcement officers to act on the belief that race or ethnicity signals a higher risk of criminality. This is the core of 'racial profiling' and it must not occur."

Here, the president is saying that even if racial profiling was shown to be effective, it would still be wrong and must not occur. So why should the president's statement not apply in even greater force to the First Amendment–protected right to freedom of religion? Since racial and ethnic profiling is allowed in cases of threats to national security or protecting border integrity, it gives the impression that officials believe ethnicity does signal a higher risk of criminality in national security cases.

Racial Profiling Destroys Trust

The MLFA in its work with American Muslim groups and organizations throughout the country can also substantiate the other main reason described by Professor Harris in his 2008 testimony:

That racial or ethnic profiling interferes with public safety (which) is that using this tactic drives a wedge between police and those they serve, and this cuts off the police officer from the most important thing the officer needs to succeed: information. . . . The police and those they serve must have a real partnership, based on trust, dedicated to the common goal of suppressing crime and making the community a good place to live and work. The police have their law enforcement expertise and powers, but what the community brings to the police—information about what the real problems on the ground are, who the predators are, and what the community really wants—can only come from the public. Thus the relationship of trust between the public and the police always remains of paramount importance.

This kind of partnership is difficult to build, but it is neither utopian nor unrealistic to strive for this kind of working relationship. In other words, this is not an effort to be politically correct or sensitive to the feelings of one or another group. Thus these trust-based partnerships are essential for public safety, and therefore well worth the effort to build. When racial profiling becomes common practice in a law enforcement agency, all of this is put in jeopardy. When one group is targeted by police, this erodes the basic elements of the relationship police need to have with that group. It replaces trust with fear and suspicion. And fear and suspicion cut off the flow of communication. This is true whether the problem we face is drug dealers on the corner, or terrorism on our own soil. Information from the community is the one essential ingredient of any successful effort to get ahead of criminals or terrorists; using profiling against these communities is therefore counterproductive.

Reports of Muslim Entrapment by the FBI Surface

Revelations of mosques being frequented and targeted by professional FBI informants and recent news stories about the FBI's "community outreach program" serving as a method for collecting information on Muslim attendees and participants have undoubtedly damaged the trust relationship with various Muslim communities.

Last month [March 2012], one FBI informant named Craig Monteilh made a dramatic confession: "I pretended to be Muslim. . . . There is no real hunt. It's fixed. It's all about entrapment." Monteilh says he did not balk when his FBI handlers gave him the OK to have sex with the Muslim women his undercover operation was targeting. Nor, at the time, did he shy away from recording their pillow talk. "They said, if it would enhance the intelligence, go ahead and have sex. So I did," Monteilh told the *Guardian* and other news outlets as he described his year as a confidential FBI informant sent on a secret mission to infiltrate Southern Californian mosques:

> It is an astonishing admission that goes to the heart of the intelligence surveillance of Muslim communities in America in the years after 9/11. While police and FBI leaders have insisted they are acting to defend America from a terrorist attack, civil liberties groups have insisted they have repeatedly gone too far and treated an entire religious group as suspicious.
>
> Monteilh was involved in one of the most controversial tactics: the use of "confidential informants" in so-called entrapment cases. This is when suspects carry out or plot fake terrorist "attacks" at the request or under the close supervision of an FBI undercover operation using secret informants. Often those informants have serious criminal records or are supplied with a financial motivation to net suspects. (excerpt from the *Guardian*)

The End Racial Profiling Act Should Be Passed

Disclosures of such egregious misconduct in conducting religious, ethnic and racial profiling cannot but seriously adversely impact the willingness of Muslims to share information with law enforcement and national security officials or to testify as witnesses. If "community policing" has long been established as most effective, the government is only hurting its ability to gather the more accurate information from unbiased members of any ethnic or religious community about ongoing crimes they spot or witness as opposed to the lesser accuracy that comes from hiring professional informants, provocateurs such as Monteilh or accepting information from opposition groups with axes to grind.

We thank you for holding this critical and timely hearing on racial profiling and the End Racial Profiling Act. Muslim Legal Fund of America is particularly concerned about many policies and programs at the national, state and local level which encourage or incentivize discriminatory law enforcement practices such as racial profiling. We believe that these practices are counterproductive, waste public resources and violate the civil and human rights of persons living in the United States.

Racial profiling occurs whenever law enforcement agents use race, religion, ethnicity, or national origin as a factor in deciding whom they should investigate, arrest or detain, except where these characteristics are part of a specific suspect description. Singling people out on the basis of their race, ethnicity, religion, national origin or perceived citizenship or immigration status is in direct breach of the founding principles of this country. Regardless of whether it takes place under the guise of the war on drugs, immigration enforcement, or counterterrorism efforts, racial profiling is always wrong. Moreover, the practice diverts precious law enforcement resources away from smart, targeted, behavior-based investigations.

"While certainly not all devout Muslims are terrorists, virtually all Islamic terrorists are devout Muslims."

The FBI Is Justified in Targeting Devout Muslims in Counterterrorism Surveillance

Robert Spencer

Robert Spencer is an author who specializes in writing about Islam from a Western perspective. He runs the blog Jihad Watch and has published several best-selling books. In the following viewpoint, Spencer expresses support for the controversial Federal Bureau of Investigation (FBI) training materials about Muslims that liberal writer Spencer Ackerman described as offensive and inflammatory in an article for Wired. *Robert Spencer argues that Islam is a religion that promotes war and violence against non-Muslims and that devout Muslims never become more tolerant. He sees a strong correlation between Muslim terrorists and devout belief, and he calls for the FBI to continue its training program as originally designed and not heed to a liberal agenda.*

As you read, consider the following questions:

1. Why does Spencer consider the Prophet Muhammad a cult leader?

2. According to the viewpoint, citing a twelfth-century Islamic writer, why must Muslims fight with non-Muslims?

3. According to the author, what is the definition of the term "Lysenkoism," and how does it apply to his argument?

The FBI [Federal Bureau of Investigation] came under fire again Wednesday [in September 2011] from hard-left journalist Spencer Ackerman in *Wired*, who has been conducting a campaign for some time to get the bureau to purge its terrorism training seminars of any hint of the truth about the global jihad and Islamic supremacism.

Ackerman reported with breathless self-righteous indignation that "the FBI is teaching its counterterrorism agents that 'main stream' [sic] American Muslims are likely to be terrorist sympathizers; that the Prophet Muhammad was a 'cult leader'; and that the Islamic practice of giving charity is no more than a 'funding mechanism for combat.' At the bureau's training ground in Quantico, Virginia, agents are shown a chart contending that the more 'devout' a Muslim, the more likely he is to be 'violent.' Those destructive tendencies cannot be reversed, an FBI instructional presentation adds: 'Any war against non-believers is justified' under Muslim law; a 'moderating process cannot happen if the Koran continues to be regarded as the unalterable word of Allah.'"

Like virtually all leftist and Islamic supremacist critiques of anti-jihad and anti-terror material, Ackerman's piece takes for granted that such assertions are false, without bothering to explain how or why. Apparently Ackerman believes that their falsity is so self-evident as to require no demonstration; unfortunately for him, however, no one else has provided any proof of this, either. And there is considerable evidence that what this FBI training material asserts is true.

Terrorist Connections to Mainstream Muslim Organizations

Are mainstream American Muslims "likely to be terrorist sympathizers"? Certainly all the mainstream Muslim organizations condemn al Qaeda and 9/11 [referring to the September 11, 2001, terrorist attacks on the United States]; however, some of the foremost of those organizations, such as the Islamic Society of North America, the Muslim American Society, the Islamic Circle of North America, the Muslim Students Association, and the Council on American-Islamic Relations [CAIR], and others, have links of various kinds to the jihad terrorist group Hamas and its parent organization, the Muslim Brotherhood, which is dedicated to imposing Islamic law around the world. A mainstream Muslim spokesman in the U.S., the Ground Zero mosque imam Feisal Abdul Rauf, refused to condemn Hamas until it became too politically damaging for him not to do so; another, CAIR's Nihad Awad, openly declared his support for Hamas in 1994. Another mainstream Muslim spokesman in this country, Reza Aslan, has praised another jihad terrorist group, Hezbollah, and called on the U.S. to negotiate with Hamas. Other mainstream Muslim spokesmen in the U.S. such as [President Barack] Obama's ambassador to the Organization of Islamic Cooperation, Rashad Hussain, and media gadfly Hussein Ibish, have praised and defended the confessed leader of another jihad terror group, Palestinian Islamic Jihad: Sami al-Arian.

Do these men and organizations represent a tiny minority of extremists that actually does not express the opinions of the broad mainstream of Muslims in this country? Maybe, but if so, they simply do not have any counterparts of comparable size or influence who have not expressed sympathy for some form of Islamic terror.

The Controversial Character of the Prophet Muhammad

Was Muhammad a "cult leader"? Certainly one definition of a cult is that members are not free to opt out if they choose to do so—and it was Muhammad who enunciated Islam's notorious death penalty for apostasy by saying, "Whoever changes his Islamic religion, then kill him." Also, there are several celebrated incidents in which Muhammad lashed out violently against his opponents, ordering the murder of several people for the crime of making fun of him—including the poet Abu 'Afak, who was over one hundred years old, and the poetess 'Asma bint Marwan. Abu 'Afak was killed in his sleep, in response to Muhammad's question, "Who will avenge me on this scoundrel?" Similarly, Muhammad on another occasion cried out, "Will no one rid me of this daughter of Marwan?" One of his followers, 'Umayr ibn 'Adi, went to her house that night, where he found her sleeping next to her children. The youngest, a nursing babe, was in her arms. But that didn't stop 'Umayr from murdering her and the baby as well. Muhammad commended him: "You have done a great service to Allah and His Messenger, 'Umayr!" (Ibn Ishaq, 674–676). Is the "Islamic practice of giving charity" no more than a "'funding mechanism for combat'"? If not, one wonders why so many Islamic charities in the United States and around the world have been shut down for funding terrorism, including what was once the largest Islamic charity in the United States, the Holy Land Foundation for Relief and Development (HLF), as well as the Global Relief Foundation (GRF), the Benevolence International Foundation (BIF), and many others.

Islamic Terrorists Justify Violence with Religious Doctrine

Is it true that "the more 'devout' a Muslim, the more likely he is to be 'violent,'" and is it also true that "moderating process cannot happen if the Koran continues to be regarded as the unalterable word of Allah"? While certainly not all devout Muslims are terrorists, virtually all Islamic terrorists are devout Muslims. In recent years, not only Osama bin Laden but also devout Muslims such as Khalid Sheikh Mohammed, would-be Times Square bomber Faisal Shahzad, Arkansas jihad murderer Abdulhakim Muhammad, and other jihad terror plotters such as Khalid Aldawsari, Baitullah Mehsud, and Roshonara Choudhry, among many others, reference Islamic teachings to justify violence against unbelievers. Just this week, Detroit underwear bomber Umar Farouk Abdulmutallab declared in court that Muslims should only be judged by the Qur'an.

Can "any war against non-believers" really be "'justified' under Muslim law"? Majid Khadduri is an Iraqi scholar of Islamic law of international renown. In his book *War and Peace in the Law of Islam*, which was published in 1955 and remains one of the most lucid and illuminating works on the subject, Khadduri says this about jihad:

> The state which is regarded as the instrument for universalizing a certain religion must perforce be an ever expanding state. The Islamic state, whose principal function was to put God's law into practice, sought to establish Islam as the dominant reigning ideology over the entire world.... The jihad was therefore employed as an instrument for both the universalization of religion and the establishment of an imperial world state.

Jihad and the Non-Muslim Poll Tax

Imran Ahsan Khan Nyazee [is] assistant professor on the Faculty of Shariah and Law of the International Islamic University in Islamabad. In his 1994 book *The Methodology of Ijtihad*, he quotes the twelfth-century Maliki jurist Ibn Rushd: "Muslim jurists agreed that the purpose of fighting with the People of the Book ... is one of two things: it is either their conversion to Islam or the payment of jizyah." Nyazee concludes: "This leaves no doubt that the primary goal of the Muslim community, in the eyes of its jurists, is to spread the word of Allah through jihad, and the option of poll tax [jizya] is to be exercised only after subjugation" of non-Muslims.

A Shafi'i manual of Islamic law endorsed by the most prestigious institution in Sunni Islam, Al-Azhar University in Cairo, says that the leader of the Muslims "makes war upon Jews, Christians, and Zoroastrians . . . until they become Muslim or else pay the non-Muslim poll tax," and cites Qur'an 9:29 in support of this idea: "Fight those who do not believe in Allah and the Last Day and who forbid not what Allah and His messenger have forbidden—who do not practice the religion of truth, being of those who have been given the Book—until they pay the poll tax out of hand and are humbled."

Are there wars against unbelievers that cannot be justified by Islamic law? Certainly. But there is also a broad mandate for such wars—broad enough to have served as a justification for wars between Muslims and non-Muslims throughout history. During World War I, the crumbling Ottoman Empire even tried to shore up support for its war against the Allies by declaring it a jihad.

The FBI Responds to Complaints About Its Training Materials

In the face of Ackerman's reports, the FBI is in full retreat. It announced after an earlier report that it had banned use of my book *The Truth About Muhammad*, which is simply a biography of Muhammad based on the earliest Muslim sources. And this latest report quickly drove the bureau further into Lysenkoism; it quickly announced late Thursday that it was dropping the latest program that Ackerman had zeroed in on as well.

Lysenkoism was ideologically biased junk science regarding biology and agriculture that was adopted as official policy by the Soviet Union under [Joseph] Stalin. The real scientists who told the truth were sent to the gulag [Soviet labor camps].

It is no surprise that in an official environment that refuses to speak about "Islam" and "terrorism" in the same sentence—a policy which must involve quite a lot of mental and verbal gymnastics when jihad terrorists start quoting Qur'an and other Islamic sources—that the truth about Islam would come under fire whenever it appears as part of counterterrorism studies. It is no surprise that in an official environment that thinks that the Muslim Brotherhood is "largely secular" and that jihad is a wholly positive interior spiritual struggle would get nervous at revelations that somewhere the truth about Islam and jihad was getting through.

As Lysenkoism grows more entrenched and the FBI's heads planted more firmly in the sand, Spencer Ackerman's responsibility for the next jihad attack in the U.S. grows apace.

Periodical and Internet Sources Bibliography

The following articles have been selected to supplement the diverse viewpoints presented in this chapter.

Ryan Devereaux	"Anti-Islam Teachings 'Widespread' in US Law Enforcement, Campaigners Warn," *Guardian*, May 11, 2012.
Abdus Sattar Ghazali	"American Muslims Seven Years After 9/11," OpEdNews.com, September 11, 2008.
Paul Harris	"FBI Islamic Training Materials Gave OK to Infringe on Targets' Civil Rights," *Guardian*, March 28, 2012.
Huffington Post	"Justice Department Considers Racial Profiling for Terror Prevention," July 3, 2008.
Michelle Malkin	"Still Handling Homeland Security with a 9/10 Attitude," MichelleMalkin.com, September 23, 2009.
Nisa Islam Muhammad	"War on Terror Is War on Islam, Says Advocate," FinalCall.com, May 28, 2008.
Nancy Murray	"Profiling in the Age of Total Information Awareness," *Race & Class*, vol. 52, no. 2, 2010, pp. 3–24.
ProCon.org	"Does the PATRIOT Act Unfairly Target Minority and Immigrant Communities?," June 4, 2008.
Niraj Warikoo	"FBI Ditches Training Materials Criticized as Anti-Muslim," *Detroit Free Press*, February 20, 2012.
Seth Freed Wessler	"How the Hunt for Bin Laden Made U.S. Muslims and Immigrants Threats," ColorLines.com, May 4, 2011.

CHAPTER 3

Is Racial
Profiling Justifiable?

Chapter Preface

As a qualitative method, racial profiling can only be as effective as the humans who use it as a tool. Some, such as the police, may use it consciously to apprehend a criminal whom the victim cannot otherwise clearly identify. Others may use racial profiling unconsciously, letting their own prejudices come into play as they avoid certain areas of a city that feel unsafe, or call the police if they see someone who is out of place and perceived as dangerous even if the individual is not doing anything blatantly suspicious. In a post–9/11 world, Arabs—especially Arab Muslims—find themselves treated with suspicion by police, security, and civilians, much as black people have for more than two hundred years in the United States. A few well-publicized cases and a general lack of knowledge about these minority groups lead to fear, which many accept as reasonable cause for precaution. These precautions include racial profiling.

Statistician William Press makes the case that racial profiling is ineffective, in a 2010 article published in the journal *Significance*. Focusing on the problem of catching terrorists at security checks in airports, Press argues that unified random sampling will catch criminals before they can act more often than racial profiling can catch such individuals. Press says racial profiling is flawed, unevenly applied, and can be overcome by terrorists who know what signifiers to avoid. Press shows that unified random sampling is robust and not susceptible to avoidance by criminals who know how to disguise themselves. Given these quantitative, mathematical tools, Press does not believe that racial profiling is effective or justified and only serves to hurt minority communities, who feel unfairly singled out based on stereotypes of criminal behavior.

In a February 2001 article for the *National Review*, John Derbyshire asserts that racial profiling has its place because if crime statistics show that black men are responsible for a majority of robberies, then it is not fair to ban police from using race in their investigations. Burt Prelutsky, writing for *The Patriot Post* in August 2012, concurs, "I believe that even God approves of racial profiling or He wouldn't have made it so easy to identify those who need to be profiled." Proponents of racial profiling, like Derbyshire and Prelutsky, argue that it makes police work more efficient, borders more secure, and streets safer.

The effectiveness and justification of racial profiling is an ongoing debate. Even if racial profiling ceases to be a tool that police use officially in their work, it is still a reality of perception among civilians. Whether it helps people detect trouble and remain safe or widens the gaps of fellowship and understanding between culturally distinct groups is discussed by the authors of the following viewpoints.

"*Racial profiling . . . disproportionately targets people of color for investigation and enforcement. The [American Civil Liberties Union] has argued that such discrimination alienates communities from law enforcement.*"

Racial Profiling Is Morally Wrong and Based on False Assumptions

James A. Kowalski

James A. Kowalski is dean of the Cathedral Church of Saint John the Divine in New York City and a regular contributor to the Huffington Post. *In the following viewpoint, Kowalski argues that racial profiling does more damage than good and is an ineffective means of controlling crime and terrorism. He quotes extensively from major voices in this debate, including Professor Bernard E. Harcourt, who presented an important paper on racial profiling in 2009; and Professor David A. Harris, who has published an influential book,* Profiles in Injustice: Why Racial Profiling Cannot Work. *Kowalski holds up the Trayvon Martin– George Zimmerman case as an example of racial profiling gone terribly wrong.*

James A. Kowalski, "Everything Wrong with Racial Profiling," *Huffington Post*, April 25, 2012. Copyright © 2012 by the Very Reverend Dr. James A. Kowalski. All rights reserved. Reproduced by permission.

As you read, consider the following questions:

1. According to Kowalski, what information is analyzed for Customer Relations Management (CRM), and how does this affect profiling?

2. As discussed in the viewpoint, what has the American Civil Liberties Union (ACLU) said about the effect of racial profiling on people of color?

3. According to Kowalski, how did the events of September 11, 2001, affect public opinion toward racial profiling?

"... God is light and in him there is no darkness at all ... if we walk in the light ... we have fellowship with one another ..."

—1 John 1:2

"The central problem is that ... the general public and most academics are entirely comfortable using the kind of generalizations, stereotypes, and profiles based on group traits that underlie racial profiling. The public supports the use of statistical discrimination across the policing and law enforcement spectrum in the United States ... [as] a matter of plain common sense. ... Truth is, statistical discrimination permeates policing and punishment in the United States today. From the use of the I.R.S. [Internal Revenue Service] Discriminant Index Function to predict potential tax evasion, to the drug-courier and racial profiles to identify suspects to search at airports and on the highways, to risk-assessment instruments to tag violent sexual predators, prediction instruments increasingly determine individual outcomes in policing, enforcement, sentencing, and correctional practices. ..."

—Bernard E. Harcourt, "Henry Louis Gates and Racial Profiling: What's the Problem?"

Prosecutors have not charged George Zimmerman with uttering a racial slur. In this obviously racially charged and tragic case, prosecutors have alleged that Zimmerman profiled

[Trayvon] Martin just before the shooting [referring to the 2012 shooting of teenager Trayvon Martin in Sanford, Florida]. Legal experts explain that profiling does not necessarily mean racial profiling. The common law enforcement practice uses perceived "facts and circumstances" to determine whether someone may be committing a crime. Most of us support efforts to identify perpetrators by analyzing crimes and the way they are committed, both to track criminals and to prevent crime. Profiling records and classifies our behaviors. As the Electronic Privacy Information Center explains:

> "This occurs through aggregating information from online and off-line purchase data, supermarket savings cards, white pages, surveys, sweepstakes and contest entries, financial records, property records, U.S. census records, motor vehicle data, automatic number information, credit card transactions, phone records (Customer Proprietary Network Information or 'CPNI'), credit records, product warranty cards, the sale of magazine and catalog subscriptions, and public records."

We now have what is called "Customer Relations Management" (CRM) or "Personalization"—a new industry—birthed by the demand for such analyses.

Racial Profiling Harms Community Relations

Racial profiling is more specific in that it disproportionately targets people of color for investigation and enforcement. The ACLU [American Civil Liberties Union] has argued that such discrimination alienates communities from law enforcement, hinders community policing efforts, and causes law enforcement to lose credibility and trust among the people they are sworn to protect and serve. They conclude that "countless people . . . live in fear [because of] a system of law enforcement that casts entire communities as suspect."

Adam Serwer, writing for *Mother Jones*, used the profiling of the Muslim community to caution a similar boomerang effect from abuse or misunderstanding within communities. As Server stated,

> "It's no secret that New York City is a huge target for terrorism ... however, the Associated Press has shown that the New York City police have responded to that threat by treating its entire Muslim community like possible suspects. That approach harms the NYPD's ability to respond to threats in the future, since American Muslims are frequently the ones who alert law enforcement to potential threats."

There Is No Statistical Support for Racial Profiling

When University of Chicago's professor of law and political science Bernard E. Harcourt presented a paper at the Malcolm Wiener [Center's] Inequality & Social Policy program at Harvard University in 2009, he discussed the racial issues concerning the arrest of Professor [Henry Louis] Gates. He suggested that the inherent racial profiling bothered many of us most. But Harcourt's warning focused beyond racial discrimination or profiling, as he argued that the underlying premises and basic mathematical assumptions are faulty, saying that:

> "... the problem with racial profiling is precisely the misguided use of statistical discrimination in situations where there are potential feedback effects. The problem is that our customary and ordinary forms of rationality, our 'odds reasoning,' our daily uses of statistical discrimination are leading us astray. Race is the miner's canary that signals—or should signal—the larger problems of statistical discrimination and profiling. And until we properly understand the problems of statistical discrimination writ large, I fear that we will make little progress on racial profiling." ("Henry Louis Gates and Racial Profiling: What's the Problem?," Bernard E. Harcourt, 2009)

Randomization Is the Only Way to Make Law Enforcement Fair for All Citizens

We should randomize policing to a far greater extent. Since the police cannot seek consent to search *every* car that speeds over the limit, it should use mechanisms that effectively randomize over the speeding population—for example, by seeking consent from every tenth driver stopped or, say, from every person driving between 85 and 90 miles per hour. Randomization may strike you as odd at first, but it is in fact simply a mechanism to extract discretion—and racial prejudice—from the process of selecting persons to search. It is merely a mechanical way to eliminate discretion. It is the best way to take discretion out of policing *without* undermining the goal of police efficiency and *while* promoting principles of justice. Randomization, it turns out, is the only way to achieve a carceral population that reflects the offending population, and it is the only way to avoid the counterproductive effect on crime rates.

Bernard E. Harcourt,
"Henry Louis Gates and Racial Profiling: What's the Problem?,"
John M. Olin Law and Economics Working Paper #482
and Public Law and Legal Theory Working Paper #277,
University of Chicago Law School, September 2009.

Racial Profiling Is Motivated by Fear

Events of Sept. 11 [referring to the September 11, 2001, terrorist attacks on the United States] recast the profiling issue. Public opinion had become strongly against racial profiling in particular. But those terrorist attacks tipped the balance toward reimagining profiling as necessary to fight terrorism. That makes the work of people like David A. Harris, professor of law and values at the University of Toledo College of Law and a Soros Senior Justice Fellow, even more important. What if racial profiling is not only morally wrong but also ineffective? Harris is considered to be one of this nation's leading authorities. His book, *Profiles in Injustice: Why Racial Profiling Cannot Work* (2003), directly challenges the assertion of law enforcement that profiling is an effective crime-fighting tool. *Publisher's Weekly*, in reviewing Harris's book wrote:

> "[Harris] analyzes how each, aside from often not passing basic legal or ethical standards, nearly always fails to discover criminals or deter crime. These conclusions are supplemented by his often surprising analysis of arrest statistics: the New York attorney general's office shows that even though more blacks than whites were stopped and frisked for concealed weapons, the arrest rate of whites for violations was actually higher, while composite profiles of convicted criminals are skewed because 54.3% of violent crimes are never reported to the police. Other studies show just how difficult it is to guess someone's race just by looking at them."

The ineffectiveness goes to catching criminals and to preventing crime. Harris added a new chapter to examine how the events of Sep. 11 impacted public opinion and policy.

Zimmerman Was Living a Vigilante Fantasy

According to the *New York Post*, George Zimmerman has dreamed of a life in law enforcement for more than a decade. A longtime neighbor, retired clergy George Hall, told reporters that Zimmerman wanted to join either the state police or the county police. "But instead of becoming a real cop, he lived out his big blue fantasy by tracking down stray dogs, 'suspicious' children and other intruders in his gated Florida community," wrote reporters [Pedro] Oliveira and [Gary] Buiso in the *New York Post*.

Now the justice system will determine what went wrong and whether or not a crime was committed. What we know for sure is that Trayvon Martin is dead. We may also learn again that the false assumptions that undergird all sorts of profiling endanger our citizens and visitors, and divide us against each other.

> *"Color profiling absent racist stereotyping and discrimination, along with other factors, amounts to justified color profiling."*

Racial Profiling Is Morally Justifiable in Certain Circumstances

J. Angelo Corlett

J. Angelo Corlett is a professor of philosophy at San Diego State University. In the following viewpoint, Corlett distinguishes between value-neutral color profiling and the discriminatory racial profiling often practiced in the United States that he terms "racist" profiling. Corlett outlines three moral justifications for color profiling and insists that individual rights must be respected, especially because people do not always understand what their rights are. In conclusion, he challenges US law enforcement to change their approach in using profiling to make it more fair and more effective.

As you read, consider the following questions:

1. How does Corlett define color profiling?

J. Angelo Corlett, "Profiling Color," *Journal of Ethics*, vol. 15, no. 1–2, June 2011, pp. 27–31. With kind permission from Springer Science+Business Media, © 2011.

2. What are the three conditions by which Corlett has determined color profiling to be morally justified?

3. For what reason does Corlett suggest that white people would be the target of color profiling for domestic terrorism in the United States?

I shall define "color profiling" as *the use of the report(s) of a suspect's skin color in order to otherwise lawfully identify and apprehend the suspect of a criminal investigation*. This definition of "color profiling" does not specify whether or not law enforcement officers know whether a crime has been committed while the profiling is happening. And there are at least two ways to construe the epistemic character of color profiling along these lines. First, color profiling might be considered wherein a crime has been known by legal authorities to have occurred or to likely occur, as noted earlier. Let us refer to this as the "narrow" sense of "color profiling." If this is what profiling color amounts to, might it ever be morally justified?

In the case wherein legal officials do not know that a crime has been committed but suspect with probable cause that it is very likely that one has been committed, such as a case of drinking and driving (witnessing a driver's vehicle swerving on the road, for instance), reliable statistical information about which ethnic or age or gender groups are more likely than others to drink and drive might be used in order to efficiently apprehend those who drink and drive. Let us refer to this as the "broad" sense of "color profiling." But is this profiling in an acceptable sense, morally speaking? What if it were the case that of all those caught drinking and driving that 90% of such offenders were middle-class suburban whites? Would it not be justified for legal authorities to set up road stops in white suburban neighborhoods in order to apprehend such offenders, and to deter others who might offend?

Is Color Profiling Ever Morally Justified?

Is either the narrow or broad sense of "color profiling" morally justified? Are both justified? If so, under what conditions would either or both be justified? I shall provide an analysis of the conditions under which both narrow and broad senses of "color profiling" are justified. They are not intended to amount to necessary and jointly sufficient conditions of morally justified color profiling.

One ought not to ignore the caution of Bernard [E.] Harcourt that such profiling is ineffective and can indeed increase and aggravate crime in society (Harcourt 2007). But if something akin to the color-conscious approach to profiling color is ever to be on track, it would appear that there are conditions under which it might be justified on moral grounds. But just what is meant here by "morally justified," and precisely what are the grounds of such justification?

By "morally justified," one might mean one of at least two things. First, one might mean that, given the evidence one possesses at the time, one is justified in doing something. This is more of a personal justification. And of course one person's moral justification in this sense may well differ from another's. Or, it might mean that one is morally justified in a more objective sense than this, wherein a certain evidential threshold is reached that would suggest that the behavior is based on a more solid knowledge claim. I suggest that one of the problems with color profiling is that this very distinction, or something like it, is conflated, suggesting to certain law enforcement officials that their personal justification to act in a certain manner is really backed by a more objective justification when it in fact is not. What is required for morally justified color profiling, as with any other form of profiling, is not mere personal justification, but that justification which satisfies the standards of a more rigorous enterprise. Along these lines, it is helpful to begin to outline some conditions that must be satisfied in order for color profiling to be morally justified in the stronger, more than mere personal, sense. This implies that color profiling is not in itself morally wrong. Rather, it is the manner in which it is employed that makes it right or wrong on moral grounds. In this way, it is much like color categorization.

Color Profiling Requires Precise Description

The following might be construed as some of the presumptive conditions of morally justified color profiling. One such condition might be that *color profiling is justified to the extent that it is not overly broad,* being inclusive of too many folk as viable suspects. While this condition appears to be true in a trivial sense, it also serves to combat racist profiling. After all, there might be racial profiling (what I call "color profiling") that does not amount to racist profiling. For the more precise the suspect description, the less likely it is that racist stereotyping might be employed in the application of the profile to apprehend the suspect. This condition rules out the tactic of, say, using Smith's suspect description because it is far too broad, inclusive of so many people so as to be unhelpful to law enforcement agencies, and overly burdening to those who fit the description should traffic stops be utilized in order to apprehend the genuine suspect. Following this rule, the description of a criminal suspect would be permissible by law enforcement to the extent that various other indicators are provided, such as color and length of hair, facial hair, height, weight, age, clothing information, etc., along with other morphological information of the suspect. But if all the description indicates of a suspect is that he is a young black male, this serves neither law enforcement nor the public well to focus energies on such a broad and virtually unhelpful description. However, it would not follow from this that if the use of the description "young black male" would in fact increase the hit rate of criminals, then the description would not be "overly broad" and would thus fulfill my first condition.

The Bias of Witness Must Be Taken into Account

Another condition of morally justified color profiling is that the *ethnic background of the witnesses from whom the profiles are drawn must be taken into account,* understanding that errors can be made at various junctures of the process of identifying the suspect. First, the fact that many US whites fear blacks out of racism (e.g., wherein blacks are feared even though there are whites in the relevant context who appear to be and indeed are just as dangerous but who are not feared) must be taken into account when a white witness identifies a suspect as being black or brown or otherwise not white. And the same might be true if the proverbial shoe were on the other foot, as it were. This is not to say that one cannot accurately describe a suspect who does not belong to their own ethnic group. Rather, it is to recognize the common errors made when one attempts to identify members of other ethnic groups, especially in criminal justice contexts, based on the "all blacks look alike" or "all whites look alike" syndrome. Whether or not this problem is based on cognitive categorization factors, or socialization, or both, it is a problem. And whether or not color profiling is morally justified seems to rest on this not being a factor in the profiling event.

Related to the second condition is that law enforcement must make sure that a given case of color profiling is reasonable under the circumstances and that "careful attention must be paid to the accuracy of the information used in making such assessments. . . ." (Kennedy 1998: 144) This is especially true since criminals might well be sufficiently clever to plant a "witness" to misidentify suspects to law enforcement in order to throw the law off track. This is true of the Smith case wherein she planted herself as the (albeit false) witness to her own crime.

Treatment of Suspects Should Be Equal, Regardless of Race

Furthermore, color profiling is morally justified to the extent that the *same sorts of law enforcement tactics that are employed in tracking down criminals be utilized regardless of ethnicity or class.* In other words, if traffic stops and check points are used to apprehend profiled suspects in, say, brown or poor neighborhoods, thereby inconveniencing residents of those neighborhoods, then the very same tactics must be utilized when seeking such suspects in, say, white or wealthier neighborhoods. Whatever legitimate methods of apprehending suspects should be employed with the same regularity and duration with as multiethnic a staff as feasible, regardless of the kind of neighborhood in which the search is conducted. Furthermore, the kinds of questions that are asked of those being investigated must be used from context to context as should be the methods of apprehension given similar contexts of suspect apprehension. In sum, the treatment of suspects under profile ought to be the same from context to context, regardless of the color of persons being profiled. This condition is intended to ensure the fairness of the inconvenience that is shared by residents of this or that neighborhood in which such searches are conducted by law enforcement. Moreover, to the extent that entire groups may be adversely affected by color profiling, then this condition ensures that nearly all such groups suffer or are inconvenienced in roughly the same ways.[1] So when there is a white serial rapist who is sought by law enforcement, then it ought not to be the case that residents of black or brown neighborhoods are targeted by profiling. Rather, it is the residents of predominantly white neighborhoods, both rich and poor, that will bear the brunt of inconvenience and such by police searches of the suspect. Furthermore, if it is US domestic terrorism in general that is to be addressed by way of color profiling, then surely white folk by the scores must be targeted in light of the fact that recent major terrorists in the

US have been white: Timothy McVeigh and Theodore Kaczynski, not to mention the historic terrorist acts of the KKK against US blacks for generations. If any folk are to suffer from color profiling, it is all or none who are to suffer, generally speaking. There is no moral room for unfairness in the search for criminal suspects. This condition will surely require the increase in public funding of law enforcement, as current funding is insufficient for such increased measures.

Is Racial Profiling Fair Because of the Net Benefits Received?

Now this third condition runs counter to what is proposed by Kasper Lippert-Rasmussen, who argues that:

> Where functioning reciprocity obtains, to deny that racial profiling is a fair means of achieving the collective good of reduced crime on the grounds that it imposes differential burdens on those subjected to it would, in effect, be to imply that collective goods can hardly ever be brought about in a way that is fair. But this is implausible. Even if functioning reciprocity does not obtain, racial profiling is fair to those subjected to it, because even they (or at least almost all of them: those who are law-abiding and perhaps even some of those who are not) will be net beneficiaries of racial profiling. At any rate, this is likely to be the case when most crimes committed by members of a particular racial group are against other members of the same group. (Lippert-Rasmussen 2006: 193)

1. This requirement also ensures that if there is unavoidable and unintentionally visited humiliation that accompanies such profiling due to public arrest and other lawful means of search and seizure, for example, that such measures of humiliation visit all relevant parties and racial groups in roughly equal terms. The concern for humiliation due to racial profiling is raised in Paul Bou-Habib, "Racial Profiling and Background Injustice" (*The Journal of Ethics*, this issue). I assume here that some humiliation experienced during criminal racial profiling is unavoidable since, for example, most people think that anyone investigated by the police is a "trouble-maker" regardless of race. But this in itself is not a sufficiently sound reason to prohibit color profiling on moral grounds. That onlookers often do misconstrue with racist bias those who are suspected, pulled over and profiled for criminal conduct is not in itself a good reason to not profile by color, other conditions of fairness obtaining.

Racial Profiling Is Justified to Prevent Crime and Catch Criminals

If an ethnic, racial, or gender description is sufficiently narrowing in a particular circumstance, it ought to be allowed as evidence for probable cause, or as justification, to initiate police activity in regard to a particular individual or group of individuals. . . .

In order to be morally justified on the basis of the description (whether ethnic, racial, gender, or otherwise in any way), the seriousness of the police activity should be commensurate with the seriousness of the crime and the probability that the description available in a given environment identifies the alleged perpetrator being sought. The courts can set those parameters, and probably different courts will have slightly different intuitions for them. But there is no reason to believe that a merely ethnic, racial, or gender description is always insufficient cause for any police activity at all.

Rick Garlikov,
"The Concept of Racial Profiling,"
September 30, 2002. www.garlikov.com.

Rights Must Be Respected

However, this position is problematic for the following reasons. First, even if it were true that "collective goods can hardly ever be brought about in a way that is fair," this would not be a problem for one who disagrees with Lippert-Rasmussen's conclusion. For it might well be the case that ethics dictates the very truth of the claim in question. Second, his statements have a clear utilitarian ring to them, one that disregards, as utilitarians so often do, the rights of those under criminal investigation (in this case, those being profiled). To

"impose differential burdens" on those subjected to color profiling just is to violate one's right to be treated as an equal, to
not be treated differently given relevantly similar circumstances, no matter what the consequences for society. (Rawls
1971: 2–5) And, contrary to Lippert-Rasmussen's claim that
"... it may be non-comprehensively unjustified not to imple-
ment racial profiling from a deontological point of view if the
type of crime that racial profiling is being used to prevent is
sufficiently grave," (Lippert-Rasmussen 2006: 203) this kind of
thinking seeks to effectively trump rights with the goal of social utility maximization. So it is essentially a rights-
disrespecting position that masquerades as a deontological
one. For the severity of a crime to be prevented is never an
excuse to trump the rights of persons to be treated as equals.
(This is not the same as treatment as an equal, often touted
by egalitarians as a right that people possess.) The same is
true of the problematic nature of Lippert-Rasmussen's assertion that such profiling would be unjustified if not implemented if a "sufficient number of people belonging to the racial group subjected to racial profiling wants these measures
to be taken." (Lippert-Rasmussen 2006: 203) Once again, the
right of all persons to be treated as equals cannot, if it is a
right at all, be trumped by the utility considerations of one's
own community. One reason why this is true is because communities can often be incorrect about the rights they truly
have or should have vis-à-vis a criminal justice context. For
instance, members of a Latino community, as much as they
might well want to rid their community of crime—even serious crime—might think that they want color profiling to occur. But when the erosion of rights happens over time and the
community experienced the impotence that rights-erosion
brings with it, that community might well have a different at-
titude toward profiling as a means to capture suspects of even
the most violent crimes. For the end of crime prevention does
not justify the means of rights-disrespecting profiling. And

this is true whether or not the harmful wrongdoings associated with color profiling amount to expressive or non-expressive ones.[2]

Unjust Profiling, Not Color Profiling, Is the Problem

So the color-blind approach to color profiling is problematic in that it seems to assume or imply that the presumptive conditions of morally justified color profiling can never be satisfied, and that it is necessarily racist to take into account normally perceived "racial" characteristics when tracking criminals. Yet such a view is hasty, as there appears to be no reason why such conditions cannot be satisfied. In principle they can be satisfied, and must be in order for color profiling to meet the morally stringent requirements of proper law enforcement. Color profiling is not necessarily racist, though in the US it has a lengthy history of abuse. While we must remain attentive to the current realities of racist law enforcement practices that must be changed due to both individual and institutional racism within law enforcement (whether it is resultant from cognitive factors within individuals or social factors external to them), (Rowe 2004) I have set forth a new paradigm that challenges law enforcement to improve its means of apprehending criminal suspects from racial to color profiling, and by recognizing that truth in the adage that where there is injustice anywhere, there is injustice everywhere. For the unjust profiling of some group harms all of us, and must be eradicated from law enforcement.

Color Profiling Is Value Neutral and Effective

In sum, I have argued for a value-neutral conception of the nature of color profiling that does not assume that it entails racist stereotyping of criminal suspects. I have set forth jointly

2. For a discussion of color profiling that can be either expressive or non-expressive, see Lever (2005).

conditions of morally justified color profiling. Color profiling absent racist stereotyping and discrimination, along with other factors, amounts to justified color profiling. Perhaps, then, we can begin to better understand what is really occurring when law enforcement targets certain segments of the population as criminal suspects. The extent to which such behavior satisfies the conditions I articulate is the extent to which the profiling of color is morally justified. But the extent to which it fails to satisfy such standards is the degree to which law enforcement has trodden on the rights of the investigated.

References

Applbaum, A.I. 1996. Response: racial generalization, police discretion, and Baysean contractualism. In *Handled with discretion*, ed. J. Kleinig, 145–157. Lanham: Rowman & Littlefield Publishers, Inc.

Boylan, M. 2007. Genetic profiling: Ethical constraints upon criminal investigation procedures. *Politics and Ethics Review* 3: 236–252.

Corlett, J.A. 1993. Rascism and affirmative action. *Journal of Social Philosophy* 24: 163–175.

Corlett, J.A. 2003. *Race, racism, and reparations*. Ithaca: Cornell University Press.

Harcourt, B.E. 2007. *Against prediction*. Chicago: The University of Chicago Press.

Kennedy, R. 1998. Race, crime, and the law. New York: Vintage.

Lever, A. 2007. What's wrong with racial profiling? Another look at the problem. Criminal Justice Ethics 26: 20–28.

Lever, A. 2005. Why racial profiling is hard to justify: a response to Risse and Zuckerman. Philosophy & Public Affairs 33: 94–110.

Lippert-Rasmussen, K. 2006. Racial profiling versus community. Journal of Applied Philosophy 23: 191–205.

McGary, H. 1996. Police discretion and discrimination. In Handled with discretion, ed. J. Kleinig, 131–144. Lanham: Rowman & Littlefield Publishers, Inc.

Rawls, J. 1971. A theory of justice. Cambridge: Harvard University Press.

Risse, M. 2007. Racial profiling: a reply to two critics. Criminal Justice Ethics 26: 4–19.

Risse, M., and R. Zeckhauser. 2004. Racial profiling. Philosophy & Public Affairs 32: 131–170.

Rowe, M. 2004. Policing, race, and racism. Devon: Willan Publishing.

> "The government's burden of justifica-
> tion for focusing upon race as a pre-
> dominate factor in the law enforcement
> process is undoubtedly a weighty one,
> unlikely to be met in most circum-
> stances."

There Is a Constitutional and Legal Basis for Opposing Racial Profiling

Jody Feder

Jody Feder is a legislative attorney with the US Congressional Research Service. In the following viewpoint, Feder discusses the Fourth and Fourteenth Amendments in the context of the constitutionality of racial profiling by law enforcement. The Fourth Amendment protects people from unreasonable search and seizure and has limited application to racial profiling cases because, Feder explains, in many situations, the police have reasons for stopping people other than or in addition to race. The Fourteenth Amendment provides for equal protection under the law and, Feder maintains, is a stronger constitutional argument against racial profiling provided the claimants can prove they

Jody Feder, "Racial Profiling: Legal and Constitutional Issues," Congressional Research Service, April 16, 2012, pp. 1–9. www.crs.gov.

have been treated with discrimination. Feder gives examples from specific cases to underline her argument that the US Constitution supports opposition to racial profiling.

As you read, consider the following questions:

1. According to Feder, what Supreme Court case established that race was, in some instances, a reason to suspect criminal activity?

2. What did the defendants in *United States v. Armstrong* accuse the prosecution of engaging in, according to the viewpoint?

3. What Supreme Court case found an Arizona police force to be engaging in intentional racial profiling during traffic stops, according to Feder?

Racial profiling is the practice of targeting individuals for police or security detention based on their race or ethnicity in the belief that certain minority groups are more likely to engage in unlawful behavior. Examples of racial profiling by federal, state, and local law enforcement agencies are illustrated in recent legal settlements and data collected by governmental agencies and private groups, suggesting that minorities are disproportionately the subject of routine traffic stops. The terrorist attacks by the Arab Muslim hijackers on September 11 [2001], and the resultant focus on persons of Middle Eastern and South Asian descent, further underscore the tension between demands of national security and the need for evenhanded law enforcement. Some argue that racial profiling is a rational and efficient method of allocating investigatory resources to safeguard the security of all. Others counter, however, that the practice is not a legitimate security measure, but diverts investigatory scrutiny from real sources of potential threat, and that where discrimination is concerned, liberty and security do not conflict. The issue has periodically attracted congressional interest, particularly with regard to existing and proposed legislative safeguards, which include the proposed End Racial Profiling Act of 2011 (H.R. 3618/S. 1670) in the 112th Congress. Several courts have also considered constitutional ramifications of the practice as an "unreasonable search and seizure" under the Fourth Amendment and, more recently, as a denial of the Fourteenth Amendment's equal protection guarantee. Furthermore, many states have laws that address racial profiling, and several major state and county law enforcement agencies, like the New Jersey State Police, have resolved charges of racial profiling by its officers by agreeing to extensive reform efforts and reporting requirements.

The US Constitution Supports Opposition to Racial Profiling

Racial profiling, or consideration of race by police and law enforcement, is a subject that the courts have reviewed on several constitutional grounds, including whether such profiling constitutes a violation of the Fourth Amendment's prohibition against unreasonable search and seizure or the equal protection guarantee of the Fourteenth Amendment. Both of these grounds are discussed in greater detail below.

The Fourth Amendment Protects People from Unreasonable Search and Seizure

The Fourth Amendment provides that "[t]he right of the people to be secure in their persons, houses, papers, and effects, against unreasonable searches and seizures, shall not be violated." In its 1968 Fourth Amendment ruling, *Terry v. Ohio,* the Supreme Court found that reasonable, articulable suspicion was sufficient grounds for a police officer to briefly stop and question a citizen. Such suspicion must not be based on the officer's "inchoate and unparticularized suspicion or 'hunch,' but on the specific reasonable inferences which he is entitled to draw from the facts in light of his experience."

Terry employed a "totality of circumstances" test to determine the reasonableness of police investigatory stops.

United States v. Brignoni-Ponce addressed the issue of race as a factor giving rise to reasonable suspicion of criminal activity. "In this case the officers relied on a single factor to justify stopping respondent's car: the apparent Mexican ancestry of the occupants." Neither this single factor nor the police officer's belief that the occupants were illegal aliens satisfied the constitutional minimum for an investigatory stop. The court conceded "[t]he likelihood that any given person of Mexican ancestry is an alien is high enough to make Mexican appearance a relevant factor." By itself, however, that factor did not support reasonable suspicion necessary for a roving stop. The court proposed a multi-factored analysis: "Officers may consider the characteristics of the area . . . ; usual patterns of traffic on the particular road, and previous experience with alien traffic." Additionally, erratic behavior and evasive acts by those under the observation of the police officer, as well as aspects of the motor vehicle, may support the reasonable suspicion necessary for an investigatory stop. . . .

"Pretextual" Stops Are Protected by the Fourth Amendment in Some Instances

A frequently criticized form of racial profiling involves the "pretextual" traffic stop—that is, detaining minority group members for routine traffic violations in order to conduct a more generalized criminal investigation. The court directly addressed the constitutionality of the practice in 1996. Defendants in *Whren v. United States* were two motorists who were charged with drug offenses based on evidence discovered after they were pulled over for pausing at a stop sign for an unusually long time, turning without signaling, and taking off at an unreasonable speed. The *Whren* court held that the Fourth Amendment is not violated when a minor traffic infraction is a pretext rather than the actual motivation for a stop by law enforcement officers. In other words, the fact that suspects were stopped for pretextual reasons did not . . . constitutionally taint the police action or evidence of drug crimes discovered as a consequence. *Whren*, however, did not hold that the officers' motivation is entirely irrelevant when probable cause for a stop is based on a traffic violation. As explained by the court, "[t]he Constitution prohibits selective enforcement of the law based on considerations such as race. But the constitutional basis for objecting to intentionally discriminatory application of laws is the equal protection clause, not the Fourth Amendment. Subjective intentions play no role in ordinary, probable-cause Fourth Amendment analysis."

In *Atwater v. City of Lago Vista*, the court appeared to reinforce *Whren* by ruling that the Fourth Amendment did not prohibit the warrantless arrest and custodial detention of a motorist for misdemeanor traffic offenses, including failure to wear a seat belt, punishable only by a fine. Citing the "recent debate over racial profiling," Justice [Sandra Day] O'Connor dissented, arguing for a Fourth Amendment principle that would require "officers' post-stop action" in such cases to be reasonable and "proportional" to the offense committed.

The Fourteenth Amendment Provides Equal Protection Under the Law

Under the Fourteenth Amendment, "[n]o state shall . . . deny to any person within its jurisdiction the equal protection of the laws." In the wake of the *Whren* decision, racial profiling may be susceptible to two different kinds of equal protection challenges. First, claimants may argue that the conduct of an individual officer was racially motivated—that the officer stopped the suspect because of race. "If law enforcement adopts a policy, employs a practice, or in a given situation takes steps to initiate an investigation of a citizen based solely upon that citizen's race, without more, then a violation of the equal protection clause has occurred." Alternatively, the defendant may argue that he was the victim of selective enforcement. Selective enforcement equal protection claims frequently focus on the policies of departments, beyond the impact of particular enforcement actions on individual defendants.

Racial Motivation Is Unlawful

Proof of discriminatory intent is an essential element of any equal protection claim. "Determining whether invidious discriminatory purpose was a motivating factor" behind a law enforcement officer's actions "demands a sensitive inquiry into such circumstantial and direct evidence of intent as may be available." The task is complicated after *Whren* because there may be an objective, nonracially motivated basis for the stop or detention. In the case of a pretextual stop, the court must take the inquiry into illicit intent to the next level by addressing the officer's reason for taking enforcement action. But if racially motivated decision making is shown, or an agency policy employs explicit racial criteria, the claimant need not demonstrate statistically that members of his racial or ethnic group were disproportionately targeted for enforcement. "[I]t is not necessary to plead the existence of a similarly situated non-minority group when challenging a law or policy that contains an express racial classification." Rather, because the policy itself establishes a direct connection between the racial classification and the defendant's enforcement action, the policy is subject to strict scrutiny under the equal protection clause.

A challenge to the specific acts of a particular police officer is not unlike a claim of racial discrimination in the use of peremptory jury challenges, which also involves the acts of a single state actor—the prosecutor—in the course of a single transaction—the selection of a jury. The Supreme Court has instructed that "all relevant circumstances" be considered in the constitutional analysis of such cases, including the prosecutor's "'pattern' of strikes against black jurors," and the prosecutor's questions and statements, which may "support or refute an inference of discriminatory purpose." Similarly, a police officer's pattern of traffic stops and arrests, his questions and statements to the person involved, and other relevant circumstances may support an inference of discriminatory purpose in this context. But, usually, statistical evidence of disparate racial impact will not alone suffice to establish an illegal racial profiling operation. . . .

Selective Enforcement of the Law Is Unlawful

Absent an overtly discriminatory policy, or direct evidence of police motivation, racial profiling claimants face additional evidentiary burdens. A claimant alleging selective enforcement of facially neutral criminal laws must demonstrate that the challenged law enforcement practice "had a discriminatory effect and that it was motivated by a discriminatory purpose." In *United States v. Armstrong*, criminal defendants sought to attack their federal firearms and drugs charges for crack cocaine as selective prosecution based on race. The Supreme Court rejected the contention because there was no showing that similarly situated defendants of another race were treated differently by criminal prosecutors. "To establish discriminatory effect in a race case, the claimant must show that similarly situated individuals of a different race were not prosecuted." A claimant can satisfy this requirement by naming an individual who was not investigated in similar circumstances or through the use of statistical or other evidence "address-[ing] the crucial question of whether one class is being treated differently from another class that is otherwise similarly situated." This latter recourse calls for a reliable measure of the demographics of the relevant population, standards for determining whether the data represents similarly situated individuals, and relevant comparisons to the actual incidence of crime among different racial and ethnic segments of the population.

Statistical Evidence Does Not Stand Alone in Proving Discrimination

This framework has been applied in a number of proceedings involving allegations of discriminatory police enforcement practices. *Armstrong* was relied upon by the Fourth Circuit in affirming the dismissal of a racial profiling action against Virginia Beach police. The district judge in *Harris v. City of Virginia Beach*, rejected statistical evidence of a "pattern, practice, or custom of racial profiling" offered by a black driver who alleged that he was stopped for driving under the influence without probable cause. Without evidence that the officer was aware of the plaintiff's identity and race before stopping his vehicle, there was no proof of illicit motivation. Moreover, even if plaintiffs could show that a disproportionate number of minorities were stopped for traffic violations, they could not prove their claim of discriminatory treatment absent a showing that similarly situated non-minority drivers were treated differently. Since no record was kept concerning stops where no citations were issued or searches conducted, the court found that plaintiffs could not meet their burden. "Statistical evidence is generally not sufficient to show that similarly situated persons of different races were treated unequally."

The Impossible Standard of the *Armstrong* Decision

Other courts have disagreed, however, and refused to apply the "similarly situated requirement" in *Armstrong* to racial profiling by law enforcement officers because the police "never have been afforded the same presumption of regularity extended to prosecutors" and because "in the civil context, . . . such a requirement might well be impossible to meet." In *United States v. Duque-Nava*, the court concurred that application of the *Armstrong* standard to racial profiling cases would require a Section 1983 claimant to make an "impossible" showing "that a similarly situated individual was *not stopped* by the

© Jeff Parker, Florida Today and the Fort Myers News-Press, and Politicalcartoons.com.

law enforcement." For this reason, in the *Marshall* decision [referring to a decision in *Marshall v. Columbia Lea Regional Hospital*], the Tenth Circuit found that discriminatory effect could be demonstrated *either* by showing a similarly situated individual, *or* by relying on statistical evidence. And in *Chavez v. Illinois State Police*, the Seventh Circuit similarly held that statistical evidence of discriminatory effect should be accepted as proof of a selective enforcement claim based on a traffic stop. . . .

Intentional Racial Profiling in Arizona Is Ruled Unlawful

In *Ortega Melendres [et al.] v. Arpaio [et al.]*, a federal district court recently certified a class action on behalf of Latino individuals in Maricopa County, AZ, finding that the plaintiffs had presented sufficient evidence that the Maricopa County Sheriff's Office had engaged in intentional racial profiling when conducting traffic stops. Among the evidence cited by the court were statements by the sheriff indicating that his officers are both authorized and encouraged to detain people based on their appearance, with specific references to racial characteristics that he asserts are hallmarks of individuals who have the "'look of the Mexican illegal.'" As a result, the court allowed the plaintiffs' Fourth and Fourteenth Amendment claims to proceed and granted a preliminary injunction enjoining the department "from detaining any person based only on knowledge or reasonable belief, without more, that the person is unlawfully present within the United States."

The Equal Protection Doctrine Forbids Racial Profiling

Apart from problems of proof, established equal protection doctrine instructs that where race or ethnicity is the sole or "predominant" factor behind the decision to stop or arrest, "strict scrutiny" requires that government demonstrate a "compelling" justification served by "narrowly tailored" means. "Strict scrutiny" is not, however, a *per se* rule of invalidity— "strict in theory is [not] fatal in fact" but instead describes an analytical framework requiring the government to demonstrate a "close fit" between any distinction in treatment of its citizens on the basis of race and a "compelling" law enforcement or national security interest. The government's burden of justification for focusing upon race as a predominate factor in the law enforcement process is undoubtedly a weighty one, unlikely to be met in most circumstances. Nonetheless, much might depend on the "totality" of circumstances, not the least of which may be the magnitude of any public safety or national security interests at stake. "In the end, . . . even when formally strict, judicial scrutiny under the equal protection clause must be ever sensitive to the circumstances in which government seeks to act and to the methods by which it seeks to achieve even its legitimate ends."

The Equitable Standing Doctrine Protects Against Repeated Poor Treatment by Police

Besides substantive proof requirements, major procedural obstacles may limit the efficacy of private actions to end racial profiling practices. First, there is the "equitable standing doctrine" that has been applied by courts to deny an individual plaintiff the legal standing to seek injunctive relief against unconstitutional police practices unless he can show a "substantial certainty" that he will suffer similar injury in the future. In *City of Los Angeles v. Lyons*, the Supreme Court reversed the grant of injunctive relief to a black motorist permanently injured by a police choke hold applied during a routine traffic stop. Notwithstanding his allegation that numerous other individuals had been injured or killed as a result of the same practice, the plaintiff had not shown that he himself was "realistically threatened by a repetition of his experience" with the LAPD [Los Angeles Police Department]. Although he had standing to assert a damages claim, said the court, the plaintiff could not obtain an injunction because it was unlikely that he again would be subject to a choke hold. Moreover, in order to show actual threat of future injury, Lyons "would have had not only to allege that he would have another encounter with the police but also to make the credible assertion . . . that all police officers in Los Angeles always choke any citizen with whom they happen to have an encounter."

The *Lyons* principle has been applied to racial profiling cases by the lower courts, which have, with some exceptions, generally denied standing for plaintiffs who seek injunctions against future police abuse while permitting claims for damages to go forward. "[I]t is important to keep in mind that these are two distinct inquiries, and that it is possible to have standing to assert a claim for damages to redress past injury, while, at the same time, not having standing to enjoin the practice that gave rise to those damages." It could be argued, however, that a damages remedy is a less effective deterrent to constitutional misconduct because individual officers are cloaked by qualified "good faith" immunity in most cases, or may be indemnified against personal liability by their public employer.

"Supporters and opponents of [Arizona Senate Bill] 1070 assume that racial profiling is unconstitutional. . . . In fact, the U.S. Supreme Court has approved the racial profiling permitted—indeed encouraged—by SB 1070."

The US Supreme Court Has Upheld the Constitutionality of Racial Profiling

Gabriel J. Chin and Kevin R. Johnson

Gabriel J. Chin is a law professor at the University of Arizona and Kevin R. Johnson is dean and a professor of law and Chicana/o studies at the University of California, Davis. In the following viewpoint, Chin and Johnson discuss the controversial aspects of Arizona Senate Bill (SB) 1070, a proposed state law about immigration. The authors point out that the US Supreme Court has previously handed down rulings in favor of racial profiling, so according to the authors, this is not the problem with the legality of SB 1070, which was challenged in a rare Department of Justice (DOJ) lawsuit. The authors call for the US and Arizona Supreme Courts to reconsider support of racial profiling for law enforcement.

As you read, consider the following questions:

1. According to Chin and Johnson, why is the Department of Justice suing the state of Arizona over SB 1070?

2. What 1975 US Supreme Court case do the authors refer to when claiming that racial profiling is lawful?

3. According to the viewpoint, in which states have people brought racial profiling cases to court over US Border Patrol conducting unlawful search and seizure?

In its challenge to Arizona's controversial immigration law last week [in July 2010], the Justice Department argues that the state law conflicts with federal law, intruding on federal power and ability to regulate immigration. For many Americans, however, the lawsuit is needed because of concerns that Arizona's legislation, SB 1070 [Senate Bill 1070, also known as the Support Our Law Enforcement and Safe Neighborhoods Act], will lead to police harassment of people, particularly those of color, who cannot prove they are in this country legally. Yet for all the controversy over those concerns, few are talking about the real legal issue underlying the law.

Supporters and opponents of SB 1070 assume that racial profiling is unconstitutional, largely because many Americans believe that it ought to be. In fact, the U.S. Supreme Court has approved the racial profiling permitted—indeed encouraged—by SB 1070.

The U.S. Supreme Court Supports Racial Profiling

In a 1975 case regarding the Border Patrol's power to stop vehicles near the U.S.-Mexico border and question the occupants about their citizenship and immigration status, *United States v. Brignoni-Ponce*, the high court ruled that the "likelihood that any given person of Mexican ancestry is an alien is high enough to make Mexican appearance a relevant factor."

In 1982 the Arizona Supreme Court agreed, ruling in *State v. Graciano* that "enforcement of immigration laws often involves a relevant consideration of ethnic factors."

Arizona's immigration law states that a "law enforcement official or agency . . . may not consider race, color or national origin in implementing the requirements of this subsection except to the extent permitted by the United States or Arizona Constitution." Although supporters of the law, including Gov. Jan Brewer (R) and other state officials, have said repeatedly that racial profiling is prohibited in its enforcement and that those charged with carrying out the law will be trained to avoid it, the fact that the legislature included this careful exception is significant.

Lawmakers took care to embrace the reliance on race permitted by cases such as *Brignoni-Ponce*. This choice deserves acknowledgment and discussion, just like that received by the rest of the law.

Border Patrol Stops Are Sometimes Racially Motivated

Brignoni-Ponce has resulted in immigration enforcement that many contend is race based and in violation of the U.S. Constitution. In case after case, in states including Florida, Iowa and New York, defendants arguing that Border Patrol stops constituted unlawful searches and seizures under the Fourth Amendment have encountered claims by the U.S. government—including the current administration—that "Mexican" or "Hispanic" appearance, along with other factors, justified an immigration stop. Border enforcement officers regularly admit in court that "Hispanic appearance" is one reason for an immigration stop.

Racial profiling results from the perceived statistical association of particular races or nationalities with undocumented immigration—the idea, in other words, that many undocumented immigrants are from Mexico. This rationale ignores the fact that the law generally requires individual suspicion to justify criminal investigation; that a "Mexican appearance" is a vague and ambiguous description and that people from Mexico bear an array of appearances.

We suspect that *Brignoni-Ponce* and its incorporation into SB 1070 have escaped the notice of many Americans because of the ways in which racial sensibilities have evolved since the 1954 ruling in *Brown v. Board of Education*. Modern American values and most of modern constitutional law are simply inconsistent with the equation of race and suspicion authorized and encouraged by *Brignoni-Ponce*. Today, being subject to questioning by law enforcement for no other reason than that others of your race, religion or national origin are supposed to commit more of a particular type of crime is nothing short of un-American.

The United States Needs a Federal Immigration Law

The federal lawsuit raises a number of questions. We think the government's claim of federal preemption is likely to prevail: There is room for one immigration law, not a 50-state patchwork of immigration laws. But the discussion should not stop there. Perhaps that is why last Friday the League of United Latin American Citizens (LULAC) filed another challenge focusing on SB 1070's potential for racial profiling. For the Arizona officials who enacted SB 1070, the next step is to repeal the part of the law that authorizes racial profiling. As for the legal system as a whole: *Brignoni-Ponce* has been exceptional and out of the constitutional mainstream since it was decided. The U.S. and Arizona Supreme Courts should reconsider the endorsement of race-based law enforcement, which is contrary to modern notions of equality in America, and conform constitutional law to the principles held dear by most Americans.

> *"Racial profiling is deeply rooted in our country's history of racial inequity and segregation. It's time to end this discrimination by passing [the End Racial Profiling Act] without delay."*

Passage of the End Racial Profiling Act Is Crucial to Provide Legal Protections for Victims

Sameera Hafiz

Sameera Hafiz is the policy director for the Rights Working Group, a coalition of more than 340 civil liberties and human rights groups. In the following viewpoint, Hafiz describes three different people who have been subjected to discriminatory racial profiling. Representatives have introduced the 2011 version of the End Racial Profiling Act, and Hafiz argues that not only is this act long overdue for implementation, but also it is needed now more than ever because of the rise in racial profiling and discrimination that is occurring in the United States following the September 11, 2001, terrorist attacks. If passed, Hafiz concludes, the act would put into place programs and procedures to educate, protect people, and provide redress.

As you read, consider the following questions:

1. According to Hafiz, what did the Philadelphia police do to Mahari Bailey that caused him to join a lawsuit against them?

2. When did the effort to pass the End Racial Profiling Act (ERPA) begin, according to the viewpoint?

3. What does the author say will also come about with the passage of the ERPA?

Police stopped Mahari Bailey, a 27-year-old black Philadelphia attorney, four times while he was driving his Range Rover in Philadelphia between 2008 and 2010. In each case, police asked to search his car. Bailey refused each time, was never charged with a crime but joined a lawsuit alleging widespread racial profiling out of frustration that these stops seemed to be based solely on his race.

Angel Castro-Torres, 23, a Latino immigrant living in Georgia, won a settlement in a civil lawsuit against two officers in Cobb County, Ga., who stopped him when he was riding his bicycle, because he looked Latino. The officers beat Castro-Torres, breaking bones in his face after questioning him about his immigration status.

Amardeep Singh, a Sikh American, had become used to additional searches every time he took a flight after 9/11 [referring to the September 11, 2001, terrorist attacks on the United States]. But on a recent trip he was asked to hold his 18-month-old son Azaad so a Transportation Security Administration (TSA) agent could search the boy and his book bag. Singh wondered how he'd explain these pat downs to Azaad once he becomes old enough to question what's happening to him.

Both houses of Congress are considering bills that would seek to prevent Bailey, Castro-Torres, Singh and millions of people of color who face the possibility of being profiled from facing such discriminatory treatment.

The End Racial Profiling Act Has Strong Support

Last week [in December 2011], Rep. John Conyers (D-Mich.) and 37 other members of Congress introduced the End Racial Profiling Act of 2011 (ERPA), H.R. 3618—a bill that would prohibit racial profiling by law enforcement at the local, state and federal levels on the basis of race, ethnicity, national origin, religion, and gender. ERPA is a companion bill to S 1670, introduced by Senator Ben Cardin (D-Md.) and nine others in the Senate in October.

Support from people impacted by the problem—particularly communities of color—is substantial. The End Racial Profiling Act should be passed without delay.

Before the September 11th terrorist attacks, an earlier version of ERPA had significant bipartisan congressional support.

The greater likelihood of African American motorists being pulled over by law enforcement became part of the national dialogue around race in the 1990s. Racial profiling garnered also great national attention following the killing of Amadou Diallo, a Guinean immigrant who was shot 19 times by New York police officers, who had no probable cause for stopping him on his Bronx street.

More than a decade ago national concern and outrage about the problem prompted federal action. In the late 1990s, President [Bill] Clinton directed federal law enforcement agencies to collect data on the race and ethnicity of those they stopped. In February 2001, President George W. Bush called for passage of legislation to prohibit racial profiling.

Discriminatory Profiling Increased After September 11, 2001

But after the September 11 attacks, support for ERPA dropped significantly. After September 11, the government adopted many policies based on mistaken theories that religious iden-

The End Racial Profiling Act Is a Crucial Step in Reclaiming Justice

Racial profiling is a violation of our fundamental principles of justice, tainting everything it touches. The persistent use of perceived race, ethnicity, religion or national origin as the basis for questioning and arrest not only weakens the legitimacy of law enforcement in the eyes of the citizens whom they are supposed to protect, but also damages our collective image in the eyes of the world. For these reasons, we urge Congress to move toward reclaiming justice by passing the End Racial Profiling Act [ERPA], which prohibits law enforcement from subjecting a person to heightened scrutiny based on race, ethnicity, religion or national origin, except when there is trustworthy information, relevant to the locality and time frame that links a person of a particular race, ethnicity, national origin or religion to an identified criminal incident or scheme. In addition to defining and explicitly prohibiting racial profiling, ERPA would also mandate training to help police avoid responses based on stereotypes and false assumptions about minorities. ERPA would also mandate data collection, authorize grants for the development and implementation of best policing practices and would require periodic reports from the attorney general on any continuing discriminatory practices. ERPA is the one legislative proposal that offers hope for a comprehensive response to this intractable problem.

Anthony D. Romero,
"Written Statement of Anthony D. Romero,
Executive Director, American Civil Liberties Union,
Submitted to the Senate Committee on the Judiciary,
Subcommittee on the Constitution, Civil Rights
and Human Rights, Hearing on 'Ending Racial Profiling
in America,'" April 17, 2012. www.judiciary.senate.gov.

tity or national origin makes a person more likely to engage in terrorism. Arab, Muslim, Middle Eastern and South Asian Americans, as well as noncitizens of those backgrounds, became more likely to face discriminatory profiling and bias, suffering unwarranted stops, interrogations and surveillance.

When police engage in racial profiling they damage the trust developed with communities of color, making it more unlikely that these communities will feel secure in contacting them.

For Latinos racial profiling became a growing problem after 9/11, as the federal government increasingly relied on partnerships with state and local police to enforce immigration law. A 2011 [Chief Justice Earl] Warren Institute [on Law and Social Policy] report showed Latinos are targeted disproportionately through the Department of Homeland Security's Secure Communities program, which involves local and state law enforcement agencies in enforcing immigration law. Although Latinos are approximately 77 percent of the undocumented population, 93 percent of those arrested through Secure Communities are Latino.

In addition to banning racial profiling, ERPA would create training programs to guard against racial profiling and civil rights abuses. The bill would mandate data collection and monitoring, create a procedure for investigating and responding to complaints of victims of racial profiling and create a private right of action that would enable victims of racial profiling to seek redress.

Racial profiling is deeply rooted in our country's history of racial inequity and segregation. It's time to end this discrimination by passing ERPA without delay.

> *"This [End Racial Profiling Act] will ac-*
> *tually increase the unfounded allega-*
> *tions of racism when drivers and offi-*
> *cers are of a different race. Racial*
> *tensions will increase, not decrease."*

The End Racial Profiling Act Is Highly Flawed and Should Not Be Passed

Frank Gale

Frank Gale has been a police officer with the Denver County Sheriff's Department for twenty-three years and is national second vice president of the Fraternal Order of Police. In the following viewpoint, Gale discusses why law enforcement agencies across the United States are opposed to passage of the End Racial Profiling Act (ERPA). The assumption that law enforcement officers are using racist tactics as a rule is deeply offensive, Gale says. He points out that the mandates of ERPA will damage legitimate police work, such as that performed by the Federal Bureau of Investigation's Behavioral Science Unit. The data collection that would be required by ERPA, Gale contends, will further burden police with work that may be unrelated to their cases

Frank Gale, "Testimony of Frank Gale, National Second Vice President, Grand Lodge, Fraternal Order of Police, on 'Ending Racial Profiling in the United States,'" Subcommittee on the Constitution, Civil Rights and Human Rights, Committee on the Judiciary, United States Senate, April 17, 2012.

and tying these requirements to the receipt of federal money could put many local police departments in jeopardy. Gale argues that ERPA only serves to emphasize race and damages relationships between law enforcement and minorities. In conclusion, he states that the individual rights of police officers must not be forgotten while securing the rights of suspects.

As you read, consider the following questions:

1. What is Gale referring to when he writes "the very premise of the bill seems at odds with common sense"?

2. On what grounds does Gale object to mandatory data collection?

3. According to Gale, will the End Racial Profiling Act make police less aware of race, or more aware?

Good afternoon, Mr. Chairman and distinguished members of the Senate Subcommittee on the Constitution, Civil Rights and Human Rights. My name is Frank Gale; I am a twenty-three-year veteran of the Denver County Sheriff's Department and currently hold the rank of captain. I am the national second vice president of the Fraternal Order of Police [FOP], which is the nation's largest law enforcement labor organization, representing more than 330,000 rank-and-file law enforcement officers in every region of the country. I am here this morning [April 17, 2012] to discuss our strong opposition to S. 1670, the "End Racial Profiling Act," introduced by Senator Benjamin L. Cardin of Maryland.

The End Racial Profiling Act Assumes the Police Use Discriminatory Profiling

I want to begin by saying very clearly that racism is wrong. It is wrong to think a person is a criminal because of the color of his skin. But it is equally wrong to think a person is a racist because of the color of his uniform. This bill provides a "solution" to a problem that does not exist, unless one believes that the problem to be solved is that our nation's law enforcement officers are racist and that our nation's law enforcement agencies, helmed by chiefs and sheriffs, are training their officers in racist policies. I do not believe this is true and do not believe that Senator Cardin or any of the cosponsors of this bill hold this view. Nonetheless, this bill, from start to finish, provides a solution to the problem of racist police officers and, speaking for the membership of the FOP, we find the bill highly offensive. The very title of the bill presumes that unlawful racial profiling is the norm in policing and Section 101 of Title I would outlaw this practice. I ask, is there anyone in this room that honestly believes there are agencies out there training their officers or allowing their officers to engage in racial profiling as a matter of policy or procedure?

The so-called practice of "racial profiling," hyped by activists, the media and others with political agendas, is one of the greatest sources of stress between law enforcement and the minority community in our nation today. The so-called practice of "racial profiling" is, in fact, only part of the larger issue. That larger issue is a mistaken perception on the part of some that the ugliness of racism is part of the culture of law enforcement. I am here today not only to challenge this perception, but refute it entirely.

Trust Between Police and Minorities Needs to Be Rebuilt

We can and must restore the bonds of trust between law enforcement and minorities; to do so requires substantial effort to find real solutions. It requires that we resist our inclination to engage in meaningless "feel good" measures that fail to address the substance of our problem. It requires that we resist using hyperbole and rhetorical excess to place blame. This legislation does both of these things and we strongly oppose it. Open and honest communication builds trust—snappy sound bites and legislative proposals with the premise that law enforcement officers are racist do not.

I do not believe that S. 1670, the "End Racial Profiling Act," will help to repair the bonds of trust and mutual respect between law enforcement and minority communities. Quite the opposite—I believe it will widen them because it was written with the presumption that racist tactics are common tools of our nation's police departments. This is wrong and is a great disservice to the brave men and women who put themselves in harm's way every day and night to keep our streets safe.

The US Constitution Already Forbids Racial Profiling

Let me explain by addressing some of the bill's specifics.

First of all, we believe the legislation unnecessarily defines and bans "racial profiling." "Racial profiling" is not a legitimate police practice employed by any law enforcement agency in the United States. The United States Supreme Court has already made it very clear that "the Constitution prohibits selective enforcement of the law based on considerations such as race," and that "the constitutional basis for objecting to intentionally discriminatory application of the laws is the equal protection clause." (*Whren v. United States*, 517 U.S. 806, 813 (1996)). Further, as one court of appeals has explained, "citizens are entitled to equal protection of the laws at all times. If law enforcement adopts a policy, employs a practice, or in a given situation, takes steps to initiate an investigation of a citizen based solely upon that citizen's race, without more, then a violation of the equal protection clause has occurred." (*United States v. Avery*, 137 F.3d 343, 355 (6th Circuit 1997)).

The United States Constitution itself prohibits "racial profiling," making federal legislation defining or prohibiting such activity unnecessary. I am sure that there is no one on this subcommittee or in the United States Senate who would disagree that our Constitution prohibits the practice of "racial profiling." And yet, here we have a bill that proposes to prohibit a practice that the highest court in the land has already ruled to be unconstitutional and which specifically calls for the "elimination" of the practice at the federal level. The very premise of the bill seems at odds with common sense.

The End Racial Profiling Act Will Damage Legitimate Police Work

Further, the FOP contends that the legislation's definition of "racial profiling" is far too broad. The bill prohibits the use of race "to any degree" in selecting individuals to be subject to even the most routine investigatory action, excepting only those situations in which race is used "when there is trustworthy information, relevant to the locality and time frame, that links a person of a particular race, ethnicity, national origin or religion to an identified criminal incident or scheme."

This means we might as well disband the Behavioral Science Unit within the Federal Bureau of Investigation (FBI), whose work includes conducting high-impact research and presenting a variety of cutting-edge courses on topics such as Applied Criminal Psychology, Clinical Forensic Psychology, Crime Analysis, Death Investigation, and Gangs and Gang Behavior. The unit's personnel are primarily supervisory special agents and experienced veteran police officers with advanced degrees in the behavioral science disciplines who focus on developing new and innovative investigative approaches and techniques to the solution of crime by studying the offender and his/her behavior and motivation. Sometimes, their profile of a suspect contains racial information, because race can and does have an impact on our psychology. In some cases, it may be the only physical description law enforcement has to go on. The profile provided by this unit in its work on the Unabomber [referring to Ted Kaczynski who carried out a nationwide bombing campaign that killed three people and injured more than twenty others] case, for example, suggested that the suspect was a white male. Generally speaking, serial killers are much more likely to be white males than any other race or gender and investigations into serial killings generally begin with this presumption despite the fact that such a presumption is not "relevant to the locality and time frame" of the crime.

The End Racial Profiling Act Is Too Strict

Under this legislation, we would be unable to use information of this kind absent a "trustworthy" eyewitness or other description or evidence of a specific suspect's race or ethnicity. This bill is very specific on this point: Law enforcement officers can *never* use race as a factor—even if it would help them to pursue an investigation, identify a suspect, prevent a crime or lead to an arrest. The proposed legislation would therefore ban a whole range of activities beyond the already unconstitutional, purely race-based activity. The legislation would also apply to customs and immigration-related enforcement activities, as well as criminal law enforcement efforts.

What does this mean to the officer on the beat? That no one will be stopped, searched or questioned no matter how suspicious the activity without a specific eyewitness account? How can good policing, proactive policing, that deters and prevents crime occur under such a severe restriction? Perhaps you will recall the wave of national criticism following the enactment of Arizona Senate Bill 1070, the Support Our Law Enforcement and Safe Neighborhoods Act. Our members in Arizona were justifiably offended with some of the assumptions made by the media, pundits, and even elected officials who insinuated or stated outright that these professional law enforcement officers will use the law as a pretext to engage in unlawful racial profiling. Honest policy differences are both healthy and expected in the public forum, but some critics are making a real habit of crossing the line. We need to stop and think about how very insulting it is to assume that law enforcement officers will engage in biased policing, as if they do not understand the concept of reasonable suspicion or probable cause. Law enforcement officers are trained in the police academy to recognize reasonable suspicion and probable cause, not to identify and harass specific racial or ethnic groups. . . .

Tying Federal Money to Training and Data Collection Is Wrong

Mr. Chairman, the Fraternal Order of Police has fought at your side in the budgetary battles with the other body over federal funding of law enforcement. We are deeply grateful for your leadership and tenacity on these issues. You know this, as do the other members of this subcommittee, because the FOP has testified before you about the due and dangerous consequences of budget cutbacks for state and local law enforcement. We have communities in which law enforcement agencies cannot respond to every call for service and others who will no longer investigate "minor" crimes. This is a tragedy and I know we will have more battles ahead, but I must ask—how can we fight that battle if we are also going to deny these funds to agencies that need them because they cannot adequately train their officers or document allegations of "racial profiling issues?"

This makes absolutely no sense. And yet, the bill mandates that *all* state and local governments collect data, pursuant to federally established standards, to determine whether "racial profiling" is taking place as a condition of receiving federal monies—even if there is no evidence or complaint that a particular agency has engaged in such activity. Noncompliance with this mandate is punishable by the withholding of federal funds. These provisions may even violate the constitutional limits of the ability of Congress to regulate state and local governments as a condition of federal funding. On a number of occasions, the Supreme Court has expressed a narrow view with respect to federal power to regulate state and local governments pursuant to Section 5 of the Fourteenth Amendment, absent substantial evidence that constitutional rights are being violated.

Data Collection Is at Odds with Disregarding Race

Mandatory data collection is also not sound policy from a public safety perspective, because it would require law enforcement officers to engage in the collection of sociological data. When you add to the list of things that police officers have to do, you are necessarily subtracting from the law enforcement mission. Police officers are supposed to prevent crime and catch crooks, not collect data for federal studies.

How can we achieve a color-blind society if policies at the federal level require the detailed recording of race when it comes to something as common as a traffic stop? Should the passenger's race be recorded? Why not? Some traffic stops do result in the arrest of the passenger. What about the officer's race? Should that be recorded so that officers can be assigned to beats based on their ethnic background? And what if the officer is unable to determine the driver's race? Will police officers now be required to ask for "driver's license, registration and proof of ethnicity, please?"

I submit to this subcommittee that we do have a problem in our nation today—the lack of trust and respect for our police officers. Police officers also have a problem in that they have lost the trust, respect and cooperation of the minority community. This is tragic because, as we have already discussed, it is minorities in our country that are most hurt by crime and violence. This bill, however, is not the solution. It will make matters worse, not better. . . .

The End Racial Profiling Act Will Only Emphasize Race

Legislation like S. 1670 *emphasizes* racial differences. It will, in fact, make police officers much more aware of race when our

The End Racial Profiling Act Denies Equal Protection Under Law

It is critically important that legitimate, nondiscriminatory police strategies that nonetheless have a disproportionate impact on one group or another not be discouraged. Alas, this bill does that in two ways. First, it mandates data collection by beat cops, which would inevitably pressure them to stop (or not stop) people in such a way that they "get their numbers right." Second, it explicitly declares that "a disparate impact on racial, ethnic, or religious minorities shall constitute prima facie evidence of a violation of this title." Note also that this provision, ironically, makes the bill itself of dubious constitutionality, since it explicitly accepts law enforcement activities that have a disparate impact on some racial, ethnic, and religious groups, but not those that have a disparate impact on others. The End Racial Profiling Act, in other words, literally denies the equal protection of the laws and uses racial profiling.

Roger Clegg, "Testimony of Roger Clegg, President and General Counsel, Center for Equal Opportunity, on 'Ending Racial Profiling in America,'" Subcommittee on the Constitution, Civil Rights and Human Rights, Committee on the Judiciary, United States Senate, April 17, 2012.

objective should be to de-emphasize the race of the suspect. Consider this scenario: A police officer stops four drivers, all of whom are black. How is that officer to respond to allegations by the fifth driver—who may be white, Asian or Latino—that they were only stopped to inoculate the officer against charges of racism. Can a case be made that the officer's decision is racially motivated? This is the exact opposite of our intent.

This bill will actually *increase* the unfounded allegations of racism when drivers and officers are of a different race. Racial tensions will increase, not decrease, if this bill's measures are given the force of law. Supreme Court Justice Antonin Scalia reminded us, "To pursue the concept of racial entitlement—even for the most admirable and benign of purposes—is to reinforce and preserve for future mischief the way of thinking that produced race slavery, race privilege and race hatred. In the eyes of government, we are just one race here. It is American." Instead of officers looking at someone as a human being, this bill would require them to make racial and cultural distinctions between the communities they serve because they know their choices will be scrutinized from that perspective by political leaders, police managers, and the federal government.

Routine Traffic Stops Will Become Complicated

A police officer who makes a stop or an arrest—no matter what that officer's racial background—must balance the constitutional rights of the suspect with their duty to guard the public safety and preserve the peace. At a time when many citizens and lawmakers are concerned with protecting their privacy and personal information, be it concerns about the REAL ID Act, voter identification laws, or cybercrime, it seems at variance with common sense and sound public policy to ask yet another representative of government, in this case, a law enforcement officer, to collect racial or other personal data and turn that data over to the federal government for analysis. Why [should] something as simple and routine as a traffic stop require such an extraordinary imposition on a driver?

Police Officers Have Rights as Citizens as Well

I also want to emphasize that no one seems to have considered that the officer is as much a citizen entitled to his or her rights as any suspect from any allegation. Unlike most professions, many rank-and-file police officers are not, particularly in employment and disciplinary matters, guaranteed their constitutional due process protections in this country. Too often, their rights are discounted. The United States Congress has actively considered legislation similar to S. 1670 for more than a decade. The last time that legislation protecting the due process rights of police officers was debated on the Senate floor? 1991.

I do not know if, let alone how, we as a nation can solve the problems of racism. But I do know what will and will not work in the profession of law enforcement. There is a mistaken perception that the ugliness of racism is part of the culture of law enforcement. It is incumbent on all of us to correct that perception. This bill was written with this mistaken perception in mind—and it reinforces it. This legislation is not good public safety policy and will not result in good policing. It will not help to rebuild the trust between law enforcement and the minority community. For these reasons, the Fraternal Order of Police strongly opposes the bill and I urge this subcommittee to reject it.

Periodical and Internet Sources Bibliography

The following articles have been selected to supplement the diverse views presented in this chapter.

John Floyd and Billy Sinclair	"Religious and Racial Profiling Justified in McCarthy Era Inspired Investigations and Tactics," *Criminal Law Blog*, September 7, 2009. www.johntfloyd.com/blog.
Sergey Kadinsky, Tom Namako, and Dan Mangan	"Taxi Big: Fair to Profile," *New York Post*, December 7, 2010.
Aaron Kearney	"Why We Need ERPA: Racial Profiling Lingers Amidst Proof of Targeting," CAIR-Chicago, August 6, 2012. www.cairchicago.org.
Daryl Lindsey	"Profiling Ruling 'Sows Seeds of Distrust and Racism,'" *Spiegel Online*, March 29, 2012. www.spiegel.de.
Heather Mac Donald	"Fighting Crime Where the Criminals Are," *New York Times*, June 25, 2010.
Heather Mac Donald	"Targeting the Police," *Weekly Standard*, vol. 16, no. 19, January 31, 2011.
Asra Q. Nomani and Hassan Abbas	"Is Racial or Religious Profiling Ever Justified?," *New York Times Upfront*, vol. 143, April 18, 2011.
Jim Rankin	"When Good People Are Swept Up with the Bad," *Toronto Star*, February 26, 2010.
Penny Starr	"DOJ Alum at Racial Profiling Hearing Calls Crimes, Out of Wedlock Births in Black Community 'Elephant in the Room,'" CNSNews.com, April 19, 2012.
Dawud Walid	"End Racial Profiling Act: A Smarter Policy," *Huffington Post*, May 3, 2012.

OPPOSING
VIEWPOINTS®
SERIES

CHAPTER 4

What Are the Consequences of Racial Profiling?

Chapter Preface

Immigration reform is hotly debated in regard to racial profiling and discrimination. US Immigration and Customs Enforcement (ICE) launched a new program to apprehend and deport violent illegal immigrants in 2008. Called Secure Communities, this program asked local law enforcement agencies, via standard reporting protocols to the Federal Bureau of Investigation (FBI), to share with ICE the names and fingerprints of people who have been arrested on suspicion of committing serious felonies. The purpose of Secure Communities is "the removal of criminal aliens, those who pose a threat to public safety, and repeat immigration violators." ICE compares the suspect identification with their own databases and has the option to take suspects into federal custody.

According to a September 2010 article in *Police Chief* by Secure Communities executive director David Venturella, ICE reportedly arrests approximately one million illegal immigrants per year who are accused of committing a crime. In the first twenty-one months of the program, 3.2 million fingerprints were submitted to ICE and 37,918 people were deported. Seventeen percent (544) of jurisdictions nationwide participated in the program. In an official report released by ICE in August 2012, the number of compliant jurisdictions had risen to 97 percent and the total number of deported criminal illegal immigrants was 159,409.

Although considered a success by ICE, Secure Communities faced significant criticism. One problem was the cost. According to a brief report in the *Houston Chronicle* shortly after the pilot program was launched in 2008, Secure Communities was expected to cost up to $1 billion, but Congress only budgeted $200 million for the first year and $150 million for the second year. Another issue, illuminated by a *Washington Post* editorial from March 2011, is that the databases used by Secure Communities do not include fingerprint information from before 2005 when ICE switched to digital fingerprints.

Many jurisdictions initially refused to get involved with the Secure Communities program because, as the *Washington Post* editorial shared, it was perceived as another form of racial profiling that strained already tenuous relations between police and immigrants. Although local police were given guidelines on when to send information to ICE, there was still a fair amount of discretion involved; discretion that could easily be termed discrimination. A September 7, 2012, *New York Times* article by Julia Preston compares the promises of Secure Communities against the realities. According to Preston, ICE has used this program to detain and deport any illegal immigrants taken into custody by police, regardless of whether or not they have been convicted of a felony. Also, Secure Communities allegedly encouraged law enforcement to profile illegal immigrants, Preston writes. Illegal immigrants accused of crimes in the United States remain stateside until their case is tried, leading to increased costs of incarceration. And when children of illegal immigrants lose their parents to jail or deportation, they become a burden on society, either entering the foster system or living homeless on the streets.

Secure Communities was not intended to criminalize immigrants, but critics argue that it has become a general deportation tool and is not being applied as originally proposed. Most shockingly, in the first year of the program, 5,880 people detained through the Secure Communities program turned out to be US citizens. The national outcry for immigration reform—from Secure Communities to Arizona's Senate Bill 1070 to the Development, Relief, and Education for Alien Minors (DREAM) Act—indicates that the United States is due for a change in how it deals with illegal immigrants. Some feel racial profiling of immigrants should be made a priority to deal with the influx of illegal immigrants. Others maintain that profiling damages minority communities through fear and disenfranchisement. The authors of the following view-points discuss further consequences of racial profiling.

"*Racial profiling has violated the principle of protecting innocent individuals by turning thousands of innocent people across the country into the victims.*"

Racial Profiling and a Misunderstanding of Probability

Key Sun

Key Sun is a psychologist, social worker, and professor of law at Central Washington University. In the following viewpoint, Sun examines the "cognitive errors" of common assumptions surrounding racial profiling. The first error he addresses is distinguishing between relative frequency and absolute frequency of attributes that people who commit crimes experience. The second error Sun discusses is the multiplication rule of probability for criminal behavior, which addresses the complexity of variables that go into the profile of a criminal. These misunderstandings mean, Sun asserts, that racial profiling, as applied in the United States, is biased and unfairly applied to many innocent people.

As you read, consider the following questions:

1. What are three variables, other than race, that can increase the possibility that an individual will commit a crime, according to the viewpoint?

2. According to Sun's discussion of the 2007 FBI Uniform Crime Report, what percentage of arrests were of Hispanics?

3. Sun concludes that racial profiling contradicts the mission of justice in the United States, citing which two specific points?

Racial profiling can be broadly defined as a practice in law enforcement based on the belief that a person's category membership (e.g., ethnicity, national origin) functions as an indicator of criminal propensity. In my previous posts on the topic, "why moral education has not reduced racial profiling (1) & (2)," I examined some cognitive root of the biased practice. The current discussion explores another type of cognitive distortions that supports racial profiling—a misunderstanding and misapplication of probability/statistics.

One of the most typical justifications that officers use for racial profiling involves the statement that "it is true that certain 'groups' are more likely to commit offenses or infractions than the others." I think that this statement suggests the confusion about basic probability and statistics concerning criminal behavior. This confusion consists of two cognitive errors:

• unawareness of the distinction between the relative frequency and the absolute frequency regarding a particular crime-prone attribute, and

• ignorance about the multiplication rule of probability for criminal behavior. Namely, failure to recognize that criminal behavior is determined by the interaction of multiple variables or factors.

Regarding the first error, research in criminology and psychology has identified numerous variables that may increase an individual tendency to commit crime. These variables range from social disorganization, dysfunctional environments, crime learning conditions, developmental problems, lack of social control, lack of education, stigmatization, cognitive deficiencies, impulsivity, childhood trauma, as well as some associated demographic variables such as gender, social class and race. The distinction between the relative frequency and the absolute frequency can be explained with the following examples:

Research has shown that people with only high school education are more likely to commit crime than people with graduate degrees. The same can be said about high impulsive persons, who are more inclined to commit crime than low impulsive persons. Let's assume that in both cases, the former are 90% and the latter are 10% in criminal propensity. The 90% statistic looks impressive but it is quite misleading. The number only represents the relative frequency of the tendency in comparison. It does not suggest that 90% of the people who have high school diplomas or are impulsive will commit crime, because the absolute frequency (the number of offenders with the attribute out of the total population with the same attribute in the United States) is extremely low, it is certainly below 5% of the total population. Another example may make the distinction more clear. Statistically, more than 80% of serial killers are white males, but it does not suggest that being a white male makes the person 80% more likely to become a serial killer, because the absolute frequency is so low.

Additionally, the official crime statistics may be problematic. According to the FBI's Uniform Crime Report (2007) on arrest by race, of all adults and juveniles arrested nationwide in 2007, 69.7% were whites, 28.2% were blacks, 1.3% were American Indians or Alaska Natives, and 0.8 were Asians or Pacific Islanders. Although the sum is 100%, there is a problem: The arrest data on Hispanic Americans, which are 15% of the U.S. population, are conspicuously missing. Someone may argue that Hispanic populations are not really a different race and their arrest data were distributed among the four groups above (are they really four "different" races)? If it is the case, it only shows the lack of precision in the crime statistics.

The second error involves the ignorance about the multiplication rule of probability for criminal behavior. To understand the rule, we can look at how it is applied to the offender profiling for serial killers. On the basis of analyzing the characteristics of known serial killers in America (e.g., Ted Bundy, Jeffrey Dahmer, Aileen Wuornos, Robert Lee Yates, and many others), researchers have developed a profile for the offenders. The offender characteristics include: White males (80%), above average intelligence, committing the first murder at the age between 24 and 40, 50% married with a stable family life and stable jobs, and a sign of cruelty to animals in childhood, among other factors.

This offender profiling has certain validity in helping law enforcement personnel to detect and investigate serial offenders, because it is based on the understanding of the multiplication rule of probability for criminal behavior. That is, the probability of a suspect as a serial killer is a product of race, gender, intelligence, marital status, childhood deviant behavior, and other factors. In other words, because the variables are independent from one another, an individual attribute alone on the list (e.g., race, intelligence) has no predictive value about the criminal likelihood of the target person. In fact, as shown in criminological research, most criminal behaviors are the product of the interaction of multiple causes and variables, rather than determined by one or two variables.

The application of the multiplication rule to predicting and detecting serial killers has limitations, because not all identified attributes on the profiling list can be generalized to all serial killers. For example, it took about 20 years to catch

Law Enforcement Unnecessarily Uses Deadly Force on African Americans

Cynthia McKinney, the former African American congresswoman and Green Party presidential candidate during last year's [2008's] elections, believes that young, unarmed black men are under siege across the USA in states such as Texas, New York, Georgia, California and Mississippi.

She called on Congress to intervene to halt these deadly law enforcement attacks against African Americans, such as the killing of the 22-year-old Oscar Grant in Oakland, California.

Grant was shot in the back and killed by a policeman while lying facedown in handcuffs on a train platform last January; or, take the case of Jessie Lee Williams who was murdered by white corrections officer, Ryan Teel, in a Mississippi jail. Mr. Teel is now serving two life sentences for his crime.

Ifa Kamau Cush, "Black People Still Easy Prey,"
New African, *August–September 2009.*

Gary Ridgway—aka the "Green River Killer," because his name came out early but police initially thought the killer was unmarried while he was married. In addition, important psychological variables about serial killers are not included in the profile.

In short, racial profiling is biased, because:

- It is based on misunderstanding the scientific theory of probability.

- It contradicts the mission of the justice system, which has two purposes: First, to punish the guilty, and second, to protect the innocent. Racial profiling has violated the principle of protecting innocent individuals by turning thousands of innocent people across the country into the victims.

- It creates a self-fulfilling prophecy, because when officers only focus on certain categories of individuals (yes, they will catch some criminals among them), they will also bypass many criminals about whom they do not do profiling.

| "*Legal scholars also support the use of race during investigations when it's one of several factors given by a victim.*"

Racial Profiling Protects Law-Abiding Citizens

Laura L. Scarry

Laura L. Scarry is a Chicago-area lawyer who represents law en-forcement in civil rights violation cases at the state and federal level. She also writes a legal column for Law Officer. *In the fol-lowing viewpoint, Scarry discusses how it is legally permissible for police officers to take race into account when a victim or eye-witness has supplied a description. She offers the case of* Brown v. City of Oneonta, *as an example. The Second Circuit Court of Appeals for New York found in favor of the city, which was being sued by more than two hundred African American residents and university students who felt they had been unfairly profiled. The Second Circuit upheld the officers' right to interview people based on the description given by a victim, Scarry reports.*

As you read, consider the following questions:

1. According to Scarry, what percentage of the State Uni-versity of New York College student body was African American?

2. Why did the police believe the assailant in the *Brown* case was an African American male, according to the viewpoint?

3. Why, according to the viewpoint, did the Second Circuit Court of Appeals say that the Oneonta police were allowed to use race in this instance?

You're on routine patrol when you're notified by dispatch that an armed robbery has just occurred at the local convenience store in your beat. The store clerk reported a description of the suspect to dispatch: a Hispanic male, wearing a red jacket and orange baseball cap. You immediately respond to the location, and as you get within three blocks of the scene, you observe a male with a dark complexion fitting the description.

Are you legally permitted to take his race into consideration in determining the basis to stop him? The answer is yes.

This is a controversial issue and some civil rights activists have asserted taking race into consideration is a form of unlawful racial profiling. Others explain it may be a form of racial profiling, but it's still permissible.

Putting aside civil rights activists, experts and political correctness, what's a street officer to legally do? The case of *Brown v. City of Oneonta* provides the backdrop for this discussion.

Alleged Discriminatory Profiling in Oneonta

In *Brown*, approximately 200 African American individuals filed a federal civil rights suit against New York State, the Town of Oneonta and the State University of New York College (SUCO) police departments as a result of their interactions with police officers during investigating an attack on an elderly woman. The issue in the case was the extent to which police may use race in their investigation of a crime.

At the time of the incident, Oneonta had approximately 10,000 full-time residents and fewer than 300 African Americans resided in town and made up only 2 percent of the SUCO student body.

In the early morning hours in the fall of 1992, a 77-year-old woman was attacked in her home. When she contacted the police, she stated she couldn't see her assailant's face, but based on the skin color of the hand and arm, the victim knew he was African American. During the struggle with the assailant, the victim also saw he had a knife and cut his hand.

The police responded, and a canine unit tracked the assailant's scent from the victim's residence toward the SUCO campus. Unfortunately, the trail was lost after several hundred yards.

The police immediately contacted SUCO and requested a list of all its male African American students. After SUCO supplied the list, police attempted to locate and question every male African American student at SUCO. When the investigation produced no results, the police conducted a sweep of Oneonta, stopping and questioning nonwhite persons on the streets to inspect their hands for cuts. In the end, more than 200 suspects were questioned, but no one was arrested. Those whose names appeared on the SUCO list and those who were stopped and questioned filed the civil rights lawsuit against the police alleging they were singled out because of their race, which violated their rights under the Fourth and Fourteenth Amendments.

Profiling Based on Witness Report Is Permissible

This case has been in litigation for more than a decade. Nonetheless, between the various court opinions in this case, a rule has emerged: When police officers receive a description that includes race as one of several descriptive factors of the suspect, the police may use race to determine who to interact

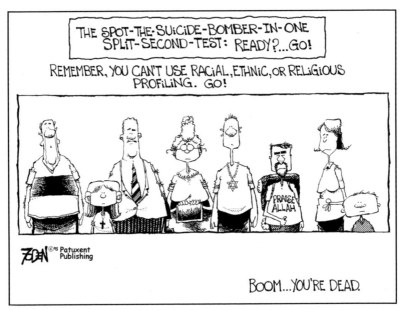

"Spot the Suicide Bomber," cartoon by Glenn Foden, www.cartoonstock.com.

with in conducting their investigation. Specifically, according to the Second Circuit Court of Appeals:

> Plaintiffs do not allege that upon hearing that a violent crime had been committed, the police used an established profile of violent criminals to determine that the suspect must have been black. Nor do they allege that the defendant law enforcement agencies have a regular policy based upon racial stereotypes that all black Oneonta residents be questioned whenever a violent crime is reported. In short, plaintiffs' faction premise is not supported by the pleadings: they were not questioned solely on the basis of race. They were questioned on the altogether legitimate basis of a physical description given by the victim of a crime.... In acting on the description provided by the victim of the assault a description that included race as one of several elements defendants did not engage in a suspect racial classification that would draw strict scrutiny. The description, which originated not with the [investigating police departments] but

with the victim, was a legitimate classification within which potential suspects might be found.

The Department of Justice Backs the Second Circuit Court of Appeals

The Department of Justice (DOJ) supports the Second Circuit's holding in *Brown*. [U]se of race or ethnicity is permitted only when the officer is pursuing a specific lead concerning the identifying characteristics of persons involved in an identified criminal activity. The DOJ even uses the facts in the *Brown* case as an illustration of the permissible use of race by the police in a description supplied by a victim.

Scholars Support the Use of Race in Specific Instances

Legal scholars also support the use of race during investigations when it's one of several factors given by a victim. For example, David A. Harris writes: "Law enforcement may properly use race in deciding whether or not reasonable suspicion exists when race comes from a description of a known suspect." In such a situation, race becomes a vital part of a particularized reason for individual suspicion. This is not only good police work; it is good for society in general.

Using *Brown* as an example, Mr. Harris asserts all of the characteristics given by the elderly victim—black male with visible cut on the hand—are valid ways of describing the suspect. According to Mr. Harris, "They are physical characteristics that one can easily recognize and use to identify someone as either looking or not looking like a particular perpetrator of a particular crime."

Brown is controversial, but the case is still good law. That said, there may be other laws, ordinances and general orders that come into play. For example, state constitutions may impose additional restrictions on the federal law governing searches and seizure and equal protection. Local ordinances and the law enforcement agencies' general orders may impose restrictions that are greater than those enunciated in the *Brown* case. In any case, it behooves law enforcement officers to check with their municipal attorney or prosecutor before taking enforcement action based on the circumstances presented in *Brown*.

> *"[Arizona Senate Bill] 1070 is the latest, albeit one of the worst, racist attacks on undocumented immigrants."*

Arizona's Immigration Law Encourages Racial Profiling

Marjorie Cohn

Marjorie Cohn is a professor at the Thomas Jefferson School of Law and a contributor to the journal JURIST. *In the following viewpoint, Cohn discusses the unconstitutionality of Arizona Senate Bill 1070, an immigration bill charged by the US Department of Justice with contravening the supremacy clause of the US Constitution. Cohn points out details of the bill that are at odds with federal statute, such as the solicitation of work and racial profiling. The bill will also be costly for the state as it loses a major source of inexpensive labor from the undocumented workers being deported, Cohn asserts. Quoting others, Cohn draws parallels with the Nazis and the internment of Japanese Americans during World War II. Even as other states are investigating similar bills, Cohn adds, civil rights and religious groups are pushing back by signing petitions and mounting protests.*

As you read, consider the following questions:

1. According to Cohn, what action can a person take if he or she feels that a municipality is not catching enough undocumented immigrants?

2. The solicitation of work is considered legal by which law, according to the viewpoint?

3. How many jobs did the Perryman Group estimate that Arizona would lose if all undocumented immigrants were deported, according to Cohn?

The conservative "states' rights" mantra sweeping our country has led to one of the most egregious wrongs in recent U.S. history. New legislation in Arizona requires law enforcement officers to stop everyone whom they have "reasonable suspicion" to believe is an undocumented immigrant and arrest them if they fail to produce their papers. What constitutes "reasonable suspicion"? When asked what an undocumented person looks like, Arizona governor Jan Brewer, who signed SB 1070 [referring to Arizona Senate Bill 1070, also known as Support Our Law Enforcement and Safe Neighborhoods Act] into law last week [in April 2010], said, "I don't know what an undocumented person looks like." The bill does not prohibit police from relying on race or ethnicity in deciding who to stop. It is unlikely that officers will detain Irish or German immigrants to check their documents. This law unconstitutionally criminalizes "walking while brown" in Arizona.

Arizona's Governor Was Swayed by Partisan Politics

Former Arizona attorney general Grant Woods explained to Brewer that SB 1070 would vest too much discretion in the state police and lead to racial profiling and expensive legal fees for the state. But the governor evidently succumbed to racist pressure as she faces a reelection campaign. Woods said,

"[Brewer] really felt that the majority of Arizonans fall on the side of, 'Let's solve the problem and not worry about the Constitution.'" The polls Brewer apparently relied on, however, employed questionable methodology and were conducted before heavy media coverage of the controversial legislation. No Democrats and all but one Republican Arizona legislator voted for SB 1070.

Undocumented immigrants in Arizona now face six months in jail and a $500 fine for the first offense—misdemeanor trespass—and an additional $1,000 fine for the second offense, which becomes a felony.

By establishing a separate state crime for anyone who violates federal immigration law, the new Arizona law contravenes the supremacy clause of the Constitution, which grants the federal government exclusive power to regulate U.S. borders.

Arizona Immigration Law Creates Frivolous Lawsuits

SB 1070 creates a cause of action for any person to sue a city, town or county if he or she feels the police are not stopping enough undocumented immigrants. Even if a municipality is innocent, it will still be forced to rack up exorbitant legal fees to defend itself against frivolous lawsuits.

The bill also makes it a misdemeanor to attempt to hire or pick up day laborers to work at a different location if the driver impedes the normal flow of traffic, albeit briefly. How many New York taxi drivers impede the flow of traffic when they pick up fares? The law also criminalizes the solicitation of work by an undocumented immigrant in a public place, who gestures or nods to a would-be employer passing by. This part of the legislation is also unconstitutional as courts have held that the solicitation of work is protected speech under the First Amendment.

The new law effectively compels Arizona police to make immigration enforcement their top priority. Indeed several law enforcement groups oppose SB 1070. The Law Enforcement Engagement Initiative, an organization of police officials who favor federal immigration reform, condemned the law, saying it would probably result in racial profiling and threaten public safety because undocumented people would hesitate to come forward and report crimes or cooperate with police for fear of being deported. The Arizona Association of Chiefs of Police also criticized the legislation, saying it will "negatively affect the ability of law enforcement agencies across the state to fulfill their many responsibilities in a timely manner"; the group believes the immigration issue is best addressed at the federal level.

Civil Rights Groups Mount a Defense

Many civil rights and faith-based organizations also oppose SB 1070. The Mexican American Legal Defense and Educational Fund (MALDEF) called the law "tantamount to a declaration of secession." The National Coalition of Latino Clergy and Christian Leaders Legal Defense Fund—which represents 30,000 evangelical churches nationwide—as well as MALDEF, the National Day Laborer Organizing Network (NDLON), and the American Civil Liberties Union (ACLU), are preparing federal lawsuits challenging the constitutionality of SB 1070.

Cardinal Roger M. Mahony of Los Angeles called the ability of officials to demand documents akin to "Nazism." Former Arizona Senate majority leader Alfredo Gutierrez said, "This is the most oppressive piece of legislation since the Japanese internment camp act" during World War II. Representative Alfredo Gutierrez (Dem.-AZ) called for a convention boycott of Arizona. The American Immigration Lawyers Association (AILA) complied. AILA is moving its fall 2010 conference, scheduled for Arizona, to another state.

Even though SB 1070 will not take effect for at least 90 days, undocumented immigrants in Arizona are terrorized by the new law. A man in Mesa, Arizona, looked around nervously as he stood on a street corner waiting for work. "We shop in their stores, we clean their yards, but they want us out and the police will be on us," Eric Ramirez told the *New York Times*.

The High Cost of Deportation

Ironically, expelling unauthorized immigrants from Arizona would be costly. The Perryman Group calculated that Arizona would lose $26.4 billion in economic activity, $11.7 billion in gross state product, and approximately 140,324 jobs if all undocumented people were removed from the state.

"This bill does nothing to address human smuggling, the drug cartels, the arms smuggling," according to Democratic senator Rebecca Rios.

"And, yes, I believe it will create somewhat of a police state," she added. "Police in Arizona already treat migrants worse than animals," said Francisco Loureiro, an immigration activist who runs a shelter in Nogales, Mexico. "There is already a hunt for migrants, and now it will be open season under the cover of a law."

SB 1070 is the latest, albeit one of the worst, racist attacks on undocumented immigrants. The federal program called 287(g) allows certain state and local law enforcement agencies to engage in federal immigration enforcement activities. But a report released earlier this month by the Department of Homeland Security Office of Inspector General found a lack of oversight and training without adequate safeguards against racial profiling.

Other States Will Follow Suit

We can expect SB 1070 to be replicated around the country as the ugly wave of immigrant bashing continues. Lawmakers

Arizona's Immigration Law Institutionalizes Racial Profiling

Every person in Arizona and states that pass [Senate Bill] 1070–like legislation will be required to carry proof of their legal status at all times or face the possibility of being detained. In practice, it will be people of color that bear the brunt of these policies.

Alex Lach,
"The Top 5 Reasons Why SB 1070 Damages America,"
Center for American Progress, June 25, 2012.
www.americanprogress.org.

from four other states have sought advice from Michael Hethmon, general counsel for the Immigration Reform Law Institute, who helped draft the Arizona law.

"SB 1070 is tearing our state into two," said Phoenix mayor Phil Gordon, who called the bill "bitter, small-minded and full of hate."

He thinks "it humiliates us in the eyes of America and threatens our economic recovery." More than 50,000 people signed petitions opposing SB 1070 and 2,500 students from high schools across Phoenix walked out of school and marched to the state capitol to protest the bill before it passed. On Sunday, about 3,500 people gathered at the capitol, chanting, "Yes we can," "We have rights," and "We are human."

President [Barack] Obama criticized SB 1070 as "misguided," saying it will "undermine basic notions of fairness that we cherish as Americans, as well as the trust between police and our communities that is so crucial to keeping us safe." He called on Congress to enact federal immigration reform.

Migrant Workers from Mexico Are Part of the US Labor Force

But Isabel Garcia, co-chair of the Coalition for Human Rights [Coalición de Derechos Humanos] in Tucson, told *Democracy Now!* that there have been more deportations under the Obama administration than in any other administration. "This administration continues to follow the flawed concept that migration is somehow a law enforcement or national security issue," she noted.

"And it is not. It is an economic, social, political phenomenon." She mentioned that NAFTA [the North American Free Trade Agreement] has displaced millions of workers in Mexico who flood into the United States.

Instead of expressing gratitude for the backbreaking work migrant laborers contribute to our society, there is an increasingly virulent strain of racism that targets noncitizens. Republican lawmakers are joining together to oppose federal immigration reform, opting instead for a "states' rights" approach where each state is free to enact its own racist law.

Let us join the voices of compassion and oppose the mean-spirited actions that aim to scapegoat immigrants. Laws like SB 1070 demean us all.

| *"The statute is neutral. It does not permit the use of race as a factor in determining who is targeted for questioning regarding immigration status."*

Arizona's Immigration Law Does Not Encourage Racial Profiling

Hans von Spakovsky

Hans von Spakovsky is a senior legal fellow in the Center for Legal and Judicial Studies at the Heritage Foundation. In the following viewpoint, Spakovsky discusses the details of the Arizona v. United States *case challenging Arizona's Senate Bill 1070, pointing out that initial reactions to the bill as racist litigation were unfounded. The bill includes language forbidding racial profiling, Spakovsky contends, making a weak case for the US government, which is instead pursuing a suit of noncompliance with the supremacy clause of the US Constitution. Arizona's SB 1070 is, in fact, more strict than federal guidelines in regard to racial profiling, according to Spakovsky. Spakovsky argues that SB 1070 supports US border protection rather than challenging*

Hans von Spakovsky, "The Arizona Immigration Law: Racial Discrimination Prohibited," Heritage Foundation Legal Memorandum, vol. 58, October 1, 2010. Copyright © 2010 by The Heritage Foundation. All rights reserved. Reproduced by permission.

federal control, and federal lawmakers should respect the fact that Arizona is only trying to catch the criminals who are breaking federal law by crossing US borders illegally.

As you read, consider the following questions:

1. According to Spakovksy, why is it that the US Department of Justice cannot sue the state of Arizona over racial discrimination in SB 1070?

2. How has Judge Susan Bolton misread the text of SB 1070 when she issued her injunctions, according to the viewpoint?

3. Approximately how many illegal immigrants live in Arizona, according to Spakovsky?

The [Barack] Obama administration has attacked the new Arizona statute that attempts to help enforce national immigration laws on several grounds and in many forms, including in federal court. Yet the incendiary claim that the state law requires or allows illegal racial profiling, repeated by various administration officials, was conspicuously *not* included in *Arizona v. United States.* The reason is quite simple: Arizona state law actually contains more stringent restrictions against racial profiling than federal guidelines published by the U.S. Department of Justice (DOJ).

Early claims by administration officials about the Arizona law were most likely intended to increase racial profiling fears since the term "racial profiling" and some form of "discrimination" were used so often. For instance, President Barack Obama and Attorney General Eric Holder each expressed grave concerns about the potentially discriminatory aspects of the law without any evidence for such a claim. It was later revealed that many administration officials who made such claims had not read the short bill, including Attorney General Holder, who admitted in response to a question from Representative Ted Poe (R-TX) that he had "not read it." Nevertheless, in an interview with Bob Schieffer, the attorney general threatened to "bring suit on that [racial profiling] basis" were the law to have a "racial profiling impact."

The U.S. Case Against Arizona Is Not Strong

Yet the United States very tellingly did not include a racial or ethnic discrimination claim in its recently filed lawsuit against Arizona. Instead, the Obama administration challenged the law on the grounds that it somehow interfered with federal immigration priorities and thus was preempted by federal immigration law. This is a very weak claim.

In essence, the federal government is arguing that if Arizona helps to enforce the immigration laws such assistance would interfere with the federal government's plan *not* to enforce them. While logically true, that is a novel type of preemption claim under the supremacy clause since the Arizona law interferes only with the federal government's enforcement *policies* (or non-enforcement policies, as the case may be) rather than with a federal law itself. Only the "Constitution, and the Laws of the United States which shall be made in Pursuance thereof; and all Treaties made, or which shall be made, under the Authority of the United States, shall be the supreme Law of the Land" under Article VI—not the policy preferences of the president.

The Attorney General Backpedaled on Accusations of Discriminatory Profiling

The attorney general stopped just short of admitting the weakness of the racial profiling argument by claiming that the lawsuit does not attack the Arizona law's potential for discrimination because the Department of Justice "wanted to go out with what we thought was our strongest initial argument." That is a laughable claim for a department with thousands of lawyers, weeks of study, and the habit of bringing every plausible claim and then some when it files suit.

As Arizona governor Jan Brewer observed, "Why would they have to hesitate, after all the comments they made, and all the outrage that they made against the bill in regards to racial profiling, that it didn't show up?" Any lawsuit filed by the Justice Department in the future on the grounds that the statute is discriminatory on its face or necessarily leads to racial profiling would be groundless. Such claims are unsustainable based on the plain text of the Arizona statute and its adherence to federal regulations and case law regarding racial profiling.

Distinguishing "Facial" from "As Applied" Challenges

Before turning to the text of the Arizona law, it is important to distinguish between claims that a law is invalid "on its face" and those that assert it could be invalid "as applied" under certain circumstances. Almost any law can be applied in a discriminatory way, and if it is, state officials should be stopped (by a civil rights lawsuit if necessary) from enforcing it that way. But in that situation, the law itself is not the problem, and it is not struck down.

Imagine an interstate highway speed limit law, which once was more tightly controlled by federal statute but is still subject to federal guidelines. If state troopers enforce it only against blacks, or twice as often against black drivers they see speeding than against other drivers, the troopers need to be enjoined. But no one would argue that we cannot or should not have speed limits because racial profiling by state troopers is possible.

This example would result in a challenge to the statute "as applied" by the state troopers to a particular group of individuals. By contrast, a facial challenge contends that the law or practice is invalid "on its face" regardless of the circumstances surrounding its possible enforcement. To prevail in this type of legal claim, the challenger generally has to prove that the law is not valid under any reasonable set of facts.

Implementation of This Law Must Be Watched Carefully

Regarding the Arizona law, the claim that some officials might enforce it in a discriminatory manner is not a fundamental challenge to the law itself. Nevertheless, the state should be sensitive to that possibility and guard against it. In fact, Arizona did take steps to amend the law immediately after passage to minimize the possibility of discriminatory application. Even so, if many state officials are not careful to follow the prohibitions on illegal racial profiling, respect for the law will diminish to the point that enforcement will be difficult and hugely unpopular, at best.

Obama administration officials' criticisms were vague, and perhaps intentionally misleading, regarding whether they believe the law is discriminatory on its face or might be enforced in a discriminatory manner. Yet there is no reason to threaten suit against a future, possible discriminatory application—at least until there was some evidence that this actually occurred, and even then, the charge should not be about the law but about the officials implementing it. Thus, the criticisms of the law made while it was being debated, soon after enactment, and before it went into effect must necessarily be interpreted as attacking the law "on its face." It is this claim that is addressed below.

The Arizona Immigration Law Forbids Racial Profiling

The new Arizona law (SB 1070 [Senate Bill 1070, or the Support Our Law Enforcement and Safe Neighborhoods Act], as amended by HB [Arizona House Bill] 2162) expressly prohibits illegal racial profiling. Only after a law enforcement official conducts a lawful stop, detention, or arrest for "any other law or ordinance of a county, city or town or this state" may an officer question a person's immigration status. To the extent that race and ethnicity are irrelevant factors in the initial *lawful* stop, detention, or arrest (and this is almost universally true), that initial contact cannot take race or ethnicity into account at all. An officer may then question the person's immigration status only if he has a "reasonable suspicion" that the person who has been stopped, detained, or arrested is an alien and is unlawfully present in the United States.

The Arizona law also specifies that local police "may not consider race, color or national origin in implementing the requirements of this subsection except to the extent permitted by the United States or Arizona Constitution." The immigration law also mandates that its provisions must be "implemented in a manner consistent with federal laws regulating immigration, protecting the civil rights of all persons and respecting the privileges and immunities of United States citizens."

The Arizona Immigration Law Does Not Discriminate

Thus, the Arizona law *prohibits* any consideration of race or national origin by local and state law enforcement officials that is not consistent with federal law. The police may not stop someone merely out of a suspicion that a person may be present in the country illegally. Additionally, law enforcement officials may not question a person's immigration status simply because that person is, or appears to be, of a certain race or ethnicity. Claims by critics that the law allows people to be stopped based on racial profiling or requires such profiling at a later stage have no basis in the law itself—it requires a reasonable suspicion of another offense before immigration status can even be considered.

Judge Susan Bolton of the United States district court for Arizona recently issued a preliminary injunction blocking the implementation of some provisions of the Arizona law as preempted by federal law. Despite the clear text of the law, Judge Bolton read it as mandating that police inquire about the immigration status of all those arrested. Judge Bolton misread the text, but even if her reading of the statute were correct, claims of racial profiling would still be unsustainable. If every person arrested had his or her immigration status checked with federal authorities, there is no discrimination because the law would then target people of every race and ethnicity. Accepting the text as written or adopting Judge Bolton's misreading of the statute both lead to the same conclusion: The Arizona law does not discriminate.

Federal Guidelines and Court Decisions Concerning Racial Profiling

What is so odd about Attorney General Holder's claim of racial discrimination is that the language of the Arizona law is in full compliance with (and in fact stricter than) the Department of Justice's own guidance on racial profiling for federal law enforcement officers. Promulgated by DOJ's Civil Rights Division in 2003, the "Guidance Regarding the Use of Race by Federal Law Enforcement Agencies" ("guidance") outlines how race may and may not be used as part of federal law enforcement procedures.

The guidance defines racial profiling as "the invidious use of race or ethnicity as a criterion in conducting stops, searches and other law enforcement investigative procedures ... premised on the erroneous assumption that any particular individual of one race or ethnicity is more likely to engage in misconduct than any particular individual of another race or ethnicity." The guidance prohibits the use of race or ethnicity in "routine or spontaneous law enforcement decisions, such as ordinary traffic stops," except in "a specific suspect description." Federal officers are permitted to use race and ethnicity as a criterion "to the extent that there is trustworthy information, relevant to the locality or time frame, that links persons of a particular race or ethnicity to an identified criminal incident, scheme or organization."

In fact, the DOJ guidance allows federal law enforcement officers engaged in border protection activities to consider race or ethnicity "to the extent permitted by the Constitution and the laws of the United States," which almost exactly parallels the language in the Arizona law. The federal standards on racial profiling "do not affect current Federal policy with respect to law enforcement activities and other efforts to defend and safeguard against threats to national security or the integrity of the Nation's borders."

Arizona Is Supporting Federal Border Protection

As the DOJ guidance states, consideration of race and ethnicity may be used to some extent in the immigration context "because enforcement of the laws protecting the Nation's borders may necessarily involve a consideration of a person's alienage in certain circumstances." Although federal agents clearly have more authority than state officials in the immigration context, by verifying the immigration status of individuals who are suspected of being in the U.S. illegally, Arizona is engaged in its duty to support the federal government in border protection.

Even if Arizona allowed officers to stop someone on suspicion of an immigration offense alone (and the Arizona law prohibits them from doing so) and race or national origin was one factor the officer took into account, the officer's actions would still be within the Department of Justice guidelines that allow federal law enforcement agencies to consider race or ethnicity to enforce federal immigration laws, as well as court precedent. As the Supreme Court said in *United States v.*

Brignoni-Ponce, while apparent Mexican ancestry of a vehicle's occupants alone could not justify stopping a car, it was one of the factors that could properly be considered by Border Patrol officers who were conducting a roving patrol close to the Mexican border. Similarly, the Sixth Circuit Court of Appeals held that, in general, an officer's consideration of race as one of many reasons in determining whether to initiate questioning was legal "as long as some of those reasons are legitimate."

Immigration Status Is a Legitimate Reason for Detention

In *Muehler v. Mena*, the Supreme Court held that the "assumption that the officers were required to have independent reasonable suspicion in order to question [Iris] Mena concerning her immigration status" was false. The police had detained Mena due to associations with an illegal gang that were discovered during her questioning. Yet Arizona's law permits questioning of people who have already been detained or arrested for other reasons *only* if the police have a reasonable suspicion about their immigration status. Thus, the Supreme Court has already upheld the right to question the immigration status of a detainee in such a situation. The First Circuit Court of Appeals also upheld as constitutional the questioning of immigration status during a traffic stop in the case of *Estrada v. [State of] Rhode Island*.

The Supreme Court ruled in another case, *Wayte v. United States*, that for illegal consideration of race to have occurred, it would have to be shown that the "enforcement system had a discriminatory effect and that it was motivated by a discriminatory purpose." Arizona houses about 460,000 illegal immigrants, and its proximity on the southern border of the United States suggests that Arizona contains a high percentage of illegal aliens who are Hispanic. The Sixth Circuit stated in *United States v. Avery* that "only in rare cases will a statistical pattern of discriminatory impact conclusively demonstrate a constitutional violation."

Arizona's Law Supports Federal Immigration Law

Thus, the possibility that Arizona's law could have a disparate impact on Hispanic aliens due to the statistical fact that the large majority of illegal aliens in Arizona are of Hispanic origin would not constitute racial discrimination. There is no evidence whatsoever that Arizona's lawmakers enacted this law to discriminate against a particular race or national origin; the evidence is that their purpose was to help enforce immigration laws and protect the state from the high cost and other negative impacts of illegal aliens. Section 1 of the law states that "the provisions of this act are intended to work together to discourage and deter the unlawful entry and presence of aliens . . . in the United States." Therefore, it cannot be shown to have a discriminatory purpose. The Arizona immigration law is fully in line with case law regarding racial profiling and the questioning of immigration status.

Illegal Immigration Is Against the Law

Illegal immigration is an ongoing violation of federal law. Arizona's new law is an attempt to address this illegal activity by helping the federal government with its enforcement efforts.

The statute is neutral. It does not permit the use of race as a factor in determining who is targeted for questioning regarding immigration status. In fact, the Arizona law prohibits racial profiling in its text and easily complies with the guidance of the Department of Justice and the opinions of the Supreme Court and lesser courts of appeal. Arizona state senator Russell Pearce, sponsor of the bill, correctly characterized the purpose of the law: "Illegal is not a race. It's a crime and in Arizona—we're going to enforce the law."

If the Obama administration files suit alleging that the Arizona law is illegal because it uses racial profiling and is discriminatory, it will also have to file suit against all of the federal law enforcement agents who follow DOJ's guidance on racial profiling in law enforcement activities. Such a suit against Arizona is completely unwarranted and would constitute litigation based on political or other improper considerations, not the rule of law.

> *"The rates of contraband found in profiling-based drug searches of minorities are typically lower, suggesting racial profiling decreases police efficiency."*

Racial Profiling Leads to Discrimination

Donald Tomaskovic-Devey and Patricia Warren

Donald Tomaskovic-Devey is in the Department of Sociology at the University of Massachusetts Amherst. Patricia Warren is in the College of Criminology and Criminal Justice at Florida State University. In the following viewpoint, Tomaskovic-Devey and Warren discuss their research into institutionalized racial discrimination, with particular focus on traffic stops and searches by police agencies around the United States. They found proof with the North Carolina State Highway Patrol that eliminating institutional bias can also eliminate racial discrimination in how often black people are searched over white people. This is important because, according to the authors, statistically speaking black people are not more likely than white people to be carrying contraband. Tomaskovic-Devey and Warren also examine the profiling of minorities in neighborhoods, concluding that the fewer black people who live in a neighborhood, the more black

Donald Tomaskovic-Devey and Patricia Warren, "Explaining and Eliminating Racial Profiling," *Contexts*, Spring 2009. Copyright © 2009 by SAGE Publications. Reprinted by permission of SAGE Publications.

drivers will be stopped by police when driving through those neighborhoods, suggesting a personal or institutional racial bias. The authors conclude with the observation that the tide of racial bias has shifted from African Americans to Hispanics and other ethnic groups that may be perceived as living in the United States illegally. The authors suggest that President Obama is uniquely situated to successfully address the issue of racial bias.

As you read, consider the following questions:

1. What have Tomaskovic-Devey and Warren found in their research encourages racial profiling within law enforcement?

2. In their study of the North Carolina State Highway Patrol, how much more often did Tomaskovic-Devey and Warren find black drivers were searched than white drivers in 1997?

3. According to the viewpoint, what is the disparity between the percentage of the US white population who think they are racist and the percentage that actually display a bias against black people?

The emancipation of slaves is a century and a half in America's past. Many would consider it ancient history.

Even the 1964 Civil Rights Act and the 1965 Voting Rights Act, which challenged the de facto racial apartheid of the post–Civil War period, are now well over 40 years old.

But even in the face of such well-established laws, racial inequalities in education, housing, employment, and law enforcement remain widespread in the United States.

Many Americans think these racial patterns stem primarily from individual prejudices or even racist attitudes. However, sociological research shows discrimination is more often the result of organizational practices that have unintentional racial effects or are based on cognitive biases linked to social stereotypes.

The same politics and practices that produce racial profiling can be the tools communities use to confront and eliminate it.

Racial profiling—stopping or searching cars and drivers based primarily on race, rather than any suspicion or observed violation of the law—is particularly problematic because it's a form of discrimination enacted and organized by federal and local governments.

In our research we've found that sometimes formal, institutionalized rules within law enforcement agencies encourage racial profiling. Routine patrol patterns and responses to calls for service, too, can produce racially biased policing. And, unconscious biases among individual police officers can encourage them to perceive some drivers as more threatening than others (of course, overt racism, although not widespread, among some police officers also contributes to racial profiling).

Racially biased policing is particularly troubling for police-community relations, as it unintentionally contributes to the mistrust of police in minority neighborhoods. But, the same politics and organizational practices that produce racial profiling can be the tools communities use to confront and eliminate it.

Profiling and Its Problems

The modern story of racially biased policing begins with the Drug Enforcement [Administration]'s (DEA) Operation Pipeline, which starting in 1984 trained 25,000 state and local police officers in 48 states to recognize, stop, and search potential drug couriers. Part of that training included considering the suspects' race.

Jurisdictions developed a variety of profiles in response to Operation Pipeline. For example, in Eagle County, Colo., the sheriff's office profiled drug couriers as those who had fast-food wrappers strewn in their cars, out-of-state license plates, and dark skin, according to the book *Good Cop, Bad Cop* by

Milton Heumann and Lance Cassak. As well, those authors wrote, Delaware's drug courier profile commonly targeted young minority men carrying pagers or wearing gold jewelry. And according to the American Civil Liberties Union (ACLU), the Florida Highway Patrol's profile included rental cars, scrupulous obedience to traffic laws, drivers wearing lots of gold or who don't "fit" the vehicle, and ethnic groups associated with the drug trade (meaning African Americans and Latinos).

In the 1990s, civil rights organizations challenged the use of racial profiles during routine traffic stops, calling them a form of discrimination. In response, the U.S. Department of Justice argued that using race as an explicit profile produced more efficient crime control than random stops. Over the past decade, however, basic social science research has called this claim into question.

The key indicator of efficiency in police searches is the percent that result in the discovery of something illegal. Recent research has shown repeatedly that increasing the number of stops and searches among minorities doesn't lead to more drug seizures than are found in routine traffic stops and searches among white drivers. In fact, the rates of contraband found in profiling-based drug searches of minorities are typically lower, suggesting racial profiling decreases police efficiency.

Racial Profiling Violates the U.S. Constitution

In addition to it being an inefficient police practice, Operation Pipeline violated the assumption of equal protection under the law guaranteed through civil rights laws as well as the 14th Amendment to the U.S. Constitution. It meant, in other words, that just as police forces across the country were learning to curb the egregious civil rights violations of the 20th century, the federal government began training state and local police to target black and brown drivers for minor traffic violations in hopes of finding more severe criminal offending. The cruel irony is that it was exactly this type of flagrant, state-sanctioned racism the civil rights movement was so successful at outlawing barely a decade earlier.

Following notorious cases of violence against minorities perpetrated by police officers, such as the videotaped beating of Rodney King in Los Angeles in 1991 and the shooting of Amadou Diallo in New York in 1999, racially biased policing rose quickly on the national civil rights agenda. By the late 1990s, challenges to racial profiling became a key political goal in the more general movement for racial justice.

The National Association for the Advancement of Colored People (NAACP) and the ACLU brought lawsuits against law enforcement agencies across the United States for targeting minority drivers. As a result, many states passed legislation that banned the use of racial profiles and then required officers to record the race of drivers stopped in order to monitor and sanction those who were violating citizens' civil rights.

Racial Bias in North Carolina Police Work Has Decreased

Today, many jurisdictions continue to collect information on the race composition of vehicle stops and searches to monitor and discourage racially biased policing. In places like New Jersey and North Carolina, where the national politics challenging racial profiling were reinforced by local efforts to monitor and sanction police, racial disparities in highway patrol stops and searches declined.

Our analysis of searches by the North Carolina [State] Highway Patrol shows that these civil rights–based challenges, both national and local, quickly changed police behavior. In 1997, before racial profiling had come under attack, black drivers were four times as likely as white drivers to be subjected to a search by the North Carolina [State] Highway Patrol. Confirming that the high rate of searches represented ra-

Profiling Immigrants for Money

To hear Zane Seipler tell it, the McHenry County Sheriff's Office [in Illinois] sees immigrants as a cash crop. In 2004, Seipler joined the office as a deputy but was fired [in 2008] after he alleged that the office is targeting Latinos—proxy for undocumented immigrants, he said—for traffic stops.

Seipler said things changed soon after the county began cooperating with the immigration agency in 2006 and started providing space for immigrant detainees at the McHenry County Jail—for $85 per detainee a day. Seipler said he began noticing the pattern that more Latino drivers were being arrested. "The goal was to keep the immigration wing packed," he said.

Seipler began keeping track of arrests. He said a small group of deputies were posting high stop numbers, and many of the individuals they were arresting were Latinos. "They find someone who looks like they are from Central America and follow them around," he said. "If they're just pulling them over to see if they have a license, that's racial profiling."

Fernando Díaz, *"Driving While Latino,"*
Chicago Report, *vol. 38, no. 2, March–April 2009.*

cial profiling, black drivers were 33 percent less likely to be found with contraband compared to white drivers. The next year, as the national and local politics of racial profiling accelerated, searches of black drivers plummeted in North Carolina. By 2000, racial disparities in searches had been cut in half and the recovery of contraband no longer differed by race, suggesting officers were no longer racially biased in their decisions to search cars.

This isn't to suggest lawyers' and activists' complaints have stopped profiling everywhere. For example, Missouri, which has been collecting data since 2000, still has large race disparities in searching practices among its police officers. The most recent data (for 2007) shows blacks were 78 percent more likely than whites to be searched. Hispanics were 118 percent more likely than whites to be searched. Compared to searches of white drivers, contraband was found 25 percent less often among black drivers and 38 percent less often among Hispanic drivers.

How Bias Is Produced

Many police-citizen encounters aren't discretionary, therefore even if an officer harbors racial prejudice it won't influence the decision to stop a car. For example, highway patrol officers, concerned with traffic flow and public safety, spend a good deal of their time stopping speeders based on radar readings—they often don't even know the race of the driver until after they pull over the car. Still, a number of other factors can produce high rates of racially biased stops. The first has to do with police patrol patterns, which tend to vary widely by neighborhood.

Not unreasonably, communities suffering from higher rates of crime are often patrolled more aggressively than others. Because minorities more often live in these neighborhoods, the routine deployment of police in an effort to increase public safety will produce more police-citizen contacts and thus a higher rate of stops in those neighborhoods.

A recent study in Charlotte, N.C., confirmed that much of the race disparity in vehicle stops there can be explained in terms of patrol patterns and calls for service. Another recent study of pedestrian stops in New York yielded similar conclusions—but further estimated that police patrol patterns alone lead to African American pedestrians being stopped at three times the rate of whites. (And, similar to the study of racial profiling of North Carolina motorists, contraband was recovered from white New Yorkers at twice the rate of African Americans.)

Patrol Patterns Are Sometimes Racially Motivated

Police patrol patterns are, in fact, sometimes more obviously racially motivated. Targeting black bars, rather than white country clubs, for Saturday-night random alcohol checks has this character. This also happens when police stop minority drivers for being in white neighborhoods. This "out-of-place policing" is often a routine police practice, but can also arise from calls for service from white households suspicious of minorities in their otherwise segregated neighborhoods. In our conversations with African American drivers, many were quite conscious of the risk they took when walking or driving in white neighborhoods.

"My son . . . was working at the country club. . . . He missed the bus and he said he was walking out Queens Road. After a while all the lights came popping on in every house. He guessed they called and . . . the police came and they questioned him, they wanted to know why was he walking through Queens Road [at] that time of day," one black respondent we talked to said.

Minorities Are Stopped by Police at a Disproportionate Rate

The "wars" on drugs and crime of the 1980s and 1990s encouraged law enforcement to police minority neighborhoods aggressively and thus contributed significantly to these problematic patterns. In focus groups with African American drivers in North Carolina, we heard that many were well aware of these patterns and their sources. "I think sometimes they target . . . depending on where you live. I think if you live in a side of town ... with maybe a lot of crime or maybe break-ins or drugs, ... I think you are a target there," one respondent noted.

These stories are mirrored in data on police stops in a midsize Midwestern city. ... Here, the fewer minorities there are in a neighborhood, the more often African Americans are stopped. In the whitest neighborhoods, African American drivers were stopped at three times the rate you'd expect given how many of them are on the road. In minority communities, minority drivers were still stopped disproportionately, but at rates much closer to their population as drivers in the neighborhood.

This isn't to say all racial inequities in policing originate with the rules organizations follow. Racial attitudes and biases among police officers are still a source of racial disparity in police vehicle stops. But even this is a more complicated story than personal prejudice and old-fashioned bigotry.

Bias Among Individual Officers Is the Source of Racial Profiling

The two most common sources of individual bias are conscious prejudice and unconscious cognitive bias. Conscious prejudice is typically, but incorrectly, thought of as the most common source of individuals' racist behavior. While some individual police officers, just like some employers or real estate agents, may be old-fashioned bigots, this isn't a widespread source of racial bias in police stops. Not only is prejudice against African Americans on the decline in the United States, but most police forces prohibit this kind of racism and reprimand or punish such officers when it's discovered. In these cases, in fact, organizational mechanisms prevent, or at least reduce, bigoted behavior.

Most social psychologists agree, however, that implicit biases against minorities are widespread in the population. While only about 10 percent of the white population will admit they have explicitly racist attitudes, more than three-quarters display implicit antiblack bias.

Studies of social cognition (or, how people think) show that people simplify and manage information by organizing it into social categories. By focusing on obvious status characteristics such as sex, race, or age, all of us tend to categorize ourselves and others into groups. Once people are racially categorized, stereotypes automatically, and often unconsciously, become activated and influence behavior. Given pervasive media images of African American men as dangerous and threatening, it shouldn't be surprising that when officers make decisions about whom to pull over or whom to search, unconscious bias may encourage them to focus more often on minorities.

These kinds of biases come into play especially for local police who, in contrast to highway patrol officers, do much more low-speed, routine patrolling of neighborhoods and business districts and thus have more discretion in making decisions about whom to stop.

Local Police May Be More Likely to Exhibit Bias

In our research in North Carolina, for example, we found that while highway patrol officers weren't more likely to stop African American drivers than white drivers, local police stopped African Americans 70 percent more often than white drivers, even after statistically adjusting for driving behavior. Local officers were also more likely to stop men, younger drivers, and drivers in older cars, confirming this process was largely about unconscious bias rather than explicit racial profiles. Race, gender, age, class biases, and stereotypes about perceived dangerousness seem to explain this pattern of local police vehicle stops.

Strategies for Changing Unconscious Bias

Unconscious biases are particularly difficult for an organization to address because offending individuals are typically unaware of them, and when confronted they may deny any racist intent.

There is increasing evidence that even deep-seated stereotypes and unconscious biases can be eroded through both education and exposure to minorities who don't fit common stereotypes, and that they can be contained when people are held accountable for their decisions. Indeed, it appears that acts of racial discrimination (as opposed to just prejudicial attitudes or beliefs) can be stopped through managerial authority, and prejudice itself seems to be reduced through both education and exposure to minorities.

For example, a 2006 study by sociologists Alexandra Kalev, Frank Dobbin, and Erin Kelly of race and gender employment bias in the private sector found that holding management accountable for equal employment opportunities is particularly efficient for reducing race and gender biases. Thus, the active monitoring and managing of police officers based on racial composition of their stops and searches holds much promise for mitigating this "invisible" prejudice.

Citizen and police review boards can play proactive and reactive roles in monitoring both individual police behavior as well as problematic organizational practices. Local police forces can use data they collect on racial disparity in police stops to identify problematic organizational behaviors such as intensively policing minority neighborhoods, targeting minorities in white neighborhoods, and racial profiling in searches.

Aggressive enforcement of civil rights laws will also play a key role in encouraging local police chiefs and employers to continue to monitor and address prejudice and discrimination inside their organizations. This is an area where the federal government has a clear role to play. Filing lawsuits against cities and states with persistent patterns of racially biased policing—whether based on the defense of segregated white neigh-borhoods or the routine patrolling of crime "hot spots"—would send a message to all police forces that the routine harassment of minority citizens is unacceptable in the United States.

Justice in the Obama Era

Given the crucial role the federal Justice Department has played in both creating and confronting racial profiling, one may wonder whether the election of President Barack Obama will have any consequences for racially biased policing.

Obama certainly has personal reasons to challenge racist practices. And given the success of his presidential campaign, it would seem he has the political capital to address racial issues in a way and to an extent unlike any of his predecessors.

At the same time, the new president has vowed to continue to fight a war on terrorism, a war often understood and explicitly defined in religious and ethnic terms. In some ways, the threat of terrorism has replaced the threat of African Americans in the U.S. political lexicon. There's evidence as well that politicians, both Democrat and Republican, have increased their verbal attacks on illegal immigrants and in doing so may be providing a fertile ground for new rounds of profiling against Hispanics in this country. So, while the racial profiling of African Americans as explicit national policy is unlikely in the Obama administration, other groups may not be so lucky.

Americans committed to racial justice and equality will likely take this as a cautionary tale. They will also likely hope the Obama administration decides to take a national leadership role in ending racial profiling. But if it does, as sociologists we hope the administration won't make the all too common mistake of assuming racial profiling is primarily the result of racial prejudice or even the more widespread psychology of unconscious bias.

> *"Racial profiling has indeed been an ugly reality for many years. But our research in several large cities finds little evidence that it continues to be a major problem."*

The Decline of Racial Profiling

Greg Ridgeway and Nelson Lim

Greg Ridgeway is director of the Center on Quality Policing and Nelson Lim is a senior demographer with the RAND Corporation. In the following viewpoint, Ridgeway and Lim argue that racial profiling is on the decline, despite the uproar of the media and public in the wake of the arrest of Harvard professor Henry Louis Gates Jr. The authors present analyses of data from major American cities such as New York City and Cincinnati that show stops and searches of black people and white people have become level. Ridgeway and Lim acknowledge that racial profiling has not been entirely eradicated, but it is a problem that is on its way out.

As you read, consider the following questions:

1. What do Ridgeway and Lim say is a key reason minorities are disproportionately stopped?

2. According to the viewpoint, what percentage of black pedestrians where stopped by New York City officers in 2006? What percentage of white pedestrians were stopped by officers in the same period?

3. How did Ridgeway and Lim's analysis of data on traffic stops of blacks and whites in Cincinnati, Ohio, compare with the New York City analysis?

President Obama called the arrest of his friend Professor Henry Gates a "teachable moment." This is a moment to learn the facts of race and policing these days. The president put it this way: "There is a long history in this country of African Americans and Latinos being stopped by law enforcement disproportionately. That's just a fact."

Racial profiling has indeed been an ugly reality for many years. But our research in several large cities finds little evidence that it continues to be a major problem.

Police departments have made tremendous progress in both policy and practice of racial profiling. Numerous states and departments have banned it, and racial profiling prevention training is commonplace. Sgt. James Crowley, the officer who arrested Gates, has taught such a class at the local police academy for five years.

It's true that minorities continue to be stopped disproportionately to their representation in the population. But this information says nothing about whether police are racial profiling. A key reason for this disparity is exposure to police.

Police regularly allocate their officers based on a neighborhood's 911 call volume. Disproportionate numbers of African Americans and Latinos live in highly segregated areas with high crime rates. As a result, they have much greater exposure to police officers than whites who live in other parts of the city. Furthermore, even though drug use is nearly equal across races, research indicates that black drug users and sellers are likelier to be involved in frequent, public drug transactions that increase the risk of police noticing them.

To address the stop disparity question more directly, RAND researchers have conducted a series of studies in Oakland, California, and Cincinnati—two cities with histories of racial tension. We found that regardless of whether officers could identify the race of the drivers in advance, the percentage of black drivers stopped remained the same. That is, even in circumstances when race couldn't be a factor in officers' stop decisions, black drivers were still stopped at the same rate.

Such findings counter the long-standing belief that merely "driving while black" is an invitation to police harassment. And so many commentators on the Gates arrest have assumed that race played a role in the incident. Norm Stamper, retired police chief of the Seattle Police Department, said, "My personal belief is that had Professor Gates been white, the outcome would have been different . . . maybe even a couple of chuckles . . . it ended up becoming a huge national issue."

It's impossible to say whether a white Gates would have been arrested. But by examining a large number of police stops, we can draw some conclusions.

We looked at 500,000 stops that New York police department officers made in 2006 and found that 4 percent of black pedestrians who were stopped were arrested. For each black pedestrian, we found white pedestrians stopped at about the same location, at about the same time of day, and suspected of the same crime. They were arrested at the same rate: 4 percent.

The pattern holds true for other outcomes: 45 percent of black pedestrians were frisked. Similar white pedestrians were frisked 42 percent of the time. Officers used physical force against 21 percent of black pedestrians and 20 percent of white pedestrians.

We completed similar analyses in Cincinnati from 2003 to 2007. Same answer. When we compare black drivers to white drivers and make sure that they are similar on when, where, and why the stops took place, we find no differences in the stop outcomes.

While we have largely moved on from the profiling of the 1990s, the kind that resulted in lengthy court oversight in New Jersey and Maryland, our research showed that racial profiling by a few problem officers in certain neighborhoods may still persist.

In New York and Cincinnati, we found a few officers with inexplicable patterns of stopping a large number of black residents. And black pedestrians stopped on Staten Island in 2006 were more likely to be searched, arrested, or have physical force used against them. But these findings are the exception rather than the rule.

The Gates arrest rekindles painful memories of police brutality, of the tragic cases of Sean Bell, Timmy Thomas, and Rodney King. But these do not negate the progress that has been made to eradicate racial profiling—even if the improvement has not been recognized by the public, especially black and Latinos, a sizable majority of whom, in a 2004 Gallup poll, believed racial profiling is widespread.

When President Obama meets with Professor Gates and Officer Crowley this evening, he could use this "teachable moment" to communicate the progress that has been made toward ending racial bias in American policing. We need the perception to catch up with the reality that racial profiling is becoming—and must be made—a thing of the past.

Periodical and Internet Sources Bibliography

The following articles have been selected to supplement the diverse views presented in this chapter.

Associated Press	"Arizona's Sheriff Arpaio Faces Allegations of Racial Profiling as Civil Trial Kicks Off," July 19, 2012.
Elisa Batista	"Racial Profiling of Immigrants Has Consequences for All Communities," FEM 2.0, July 21, 2012. www.fem2pt0.com.
Roy Eidelson	"Immigration Reform, Yes—Scapegoating and Racial Profiling, No," *Psychology Today*, May 13, 2010.
Ella Baker Center for Human Rights	"Heal the Streets 2011 Report: What Are the Causes and Effects of Racial Profiling, and What Can We Do About It?," 2011.
Alan Gomez	"Racial Profiling Difficult to Prove, Experts Say," *USA Today*, July 11, 2012.
Devon Johnson et al.	"Attitudes Toward the Use of Racial/Ethnic Profiling to Prevent Crime and Terrorism," *Criminal Justice Policy Review*, December 2011.
Michael Martinez and Mariano Castillo	"What's Next in Arizona Immigration Battle?," CNN.com, September 6, 2012.
Helen Michell	"Police Abuse, Harassment, Discrimination & Racial Profiling of Indigenous Natives Continues," RadicalPress.com, February 27, 2011.
Todd A. Smith	"The Consequences of Racial Profiling: Driving While Black: Part II," *Regal Magazine*, January 8, 2009.
Amy Napier Viteri	"Customer: Apple Store Denied Me iPad for Speaking Farsi," WSBTV.com, June 18, 2012.

For Further Discussion

Chapter 1

1. Earl Ofari Hutchinson and Jack Dunphy disagree on the prevalence of racial profiling in contemporary society. What kind of evidence does each writer provide, and are their arguments comparable? Why or why not? Do either of these viewpoints make you think differently about the existence of racial profiling? What further work needs to be done to prove one side or the other?

2. The use of affirmative action in university admissions has been challenged in recent years as a type of racial profiling. After reading the viewpoints by Elvin Lim and Tim Wise, do you agree or disagree that affirmative action is a type of racial profiling? Explain.

3. According to William Covington, Democratic legislators predicted the abuse of stand your ground laws as he argues has occurred in the Trayvon Martin shooting. After reading the viewpoints by Covington and Scott Spiegel, do you think Florida's stand your ground law applies to the Trayvon Martin case? Why or why not?

Chapter 2

1. Selwyn Duke argues for the profiling of Arab Muslims in airports because they fit the description of a terrorist, whereas Kamalakar Duvvuru argues that this type of terrorist profiling is too simplistic. Which point of view do you find more compelling, and why? Are terrorists usually Arab Muslims, or are there others who could slip through the cracks of this type of airport security screening? Do you favor the current method of screening of all passengers, or should another method be applied to airport security? Explain your reasoning.

2. Sahar Aziz discusses the disenfranchisement of Muslims from law enforcement as a result of the Federal Bureau of Investigation infiltrating and spying on the activities of mosques and Muslim community groups. Do you believe this surveillance is necessary, or is it doing more harm than good? Explain.

3. Research the term Lysenkoism, used by viewpoint author Robert Spencer. Do you agree with this argument that Spencer's opposition is engaging in Lysenkoism? Do you think Spencer is himself engaging in Lysenkosim? Why or why not?

Chapter 3

1. J. Angelo Corlett argues for profiling under very specific guidelines. Do you believe these guidelines are already in use? Are these guidelines realistic? Do you think the application of Corlett's version of color profiling will be acceptable to minorities who decry discriminatory racial profiling? Explain your answers.

2. As pointed out by Jody Feder, the US Constitution effectively bans racial profiling through the Fourth and Fourteenth Amendments. What rights do these amendments protect, and how do those protections apply to racial profiling? Do you think there is still a loophole through which law enforcement officers could legally use racial profiling in their investigations? Why or why not?

3. Will the End Racial Profiling Act be beneficial to society as a means of reparation and equitable treatment, or will it harm society by unduly hampering the efforts of law enforcement to maintain safety? Who do you think makes a more compelling argument—Sameera Hafiz or Frank Gale? If both arguments have merits, what third option do you think is possible as a compromise between both sides of the issue?

Chapter 4

1. According to Key Sun, what are three ways that racial pro-filing is biased? Do any of these issues of bias apply to the *Brown v. City of Oneonta* case described by Laura L. Scarry? Why or why not? How do you think problems of bias can be overcome?

2. Hans von Spakovsky's argument that Arizona's Senate Bill 1070 expressly forbids racial profiling has been refuted by Marjorie Cohn. One writer is arguing the letter of the law and the other is arguing the practice of that law. Do you think that either writer is painting a more accurate picture than the other, or does the truth lay somewhere in be-tween? Do you think SB 1070 will be harmful to the state of Arizona or to the immigrants who live there? Why or why not?

3. Greg Ridgeway and Nelson Lim believe that racial profil-ing is a thing of the past. What evidence do they present to support this argument? How does their argument com-pare to that of Donald Tomaskovic-Devey and Patricia Warren? If racial profiling is a thing of the past, what could be happening to people who complain that they have been profiled? Is there some other related problem in society that needs to be resolved? Explain.

Organizations to Contact

The editors have compiled the following list of organizations concerned with the issues debated in this book. The descriptions are derived from materials provided by the organizations. All have publications or information available for interested readers. The list was compiled on the date of publication of the present volume; the information provided here may change. Be aware that many organizations take several weeks or longer to respond to inquiries, so allow as much time as possible.

American Civil Liberties Union (ACLU)
125 Broad Street, 18th Floor, New York, NY   10004
(212) 549-2500
website: www.aclu.org

The American Civil Liberties Union (ACLU) works to preserve freedoms of expression and religious practice, as well as rights to privacy, due process, and equal protection under the law. It provides free legal services to those whose rights have been violated. The ACLU website offers an array of policy statements, pamphlets, and fact sheets on civil rights issues.

Amnesty International USA
5 Penn Plaza, New York, NY   10001
(212) 807-8400 • fax: (212) 627-1451
website: www.amnestyusa.org

Founded in 1961, Amnesty International is a grassroots activist organization that aims to free all nonviolent people who have been imprisoned because of their beliefs, ethnic origin, race, or gender. Amnesty International USA makes its reports, press releases, and fact sheets available through its website, including the report "Threat and Humiliation: Racial Profiling, National Security, and Human Rights in the United States."

Cato Institute

1000 Massachusetts Avenue NW
Washington, DC   20001-5403
(202) 842-0200 • fax: (202) 842-3490
website: www.cato.org

The Cato Institute is a libertarian public policy research foundation dedicated to limiting the role of government and protecting individual liberties. It publishes the quarterly magazine *Regulation*, the bimonthly *Cato Policy Report*, and numerous policy papers and articles.

Center for Immigration Studies

1629 K Street NW, Suite 600, Washington, DC   20006
(202) 466-8185 • fax: (202) 466-8076
website: www.cis.org

The Center for Immigration Studies is a nonprofit institute dedicated to research and analysis of the economic, social, and demographic impacts of immigration on the United States. Founded in 1985, the center aims to expand public support for immigration policy that is both pro-immigrant and low immigration. The center's research and reports are available on its website.

Council on American-Islamic Relations (CAIR)

453 New Jersey Avenue SE, Washington, DC   20003
(202) 488-8787 • fax: (202) 488-0833
website: www.cair.com

The Council on American-Islamic Relations (CAIR) is a Muslim civil liberties and advocacy group focused on both bridging the gap between Muslim and non-Muslim Americans, as well as protecting the rights of Muslims in the United States. CAIR regularly meets and works with law enforcement and members of the federal, state, and local governments in order to facilitate communication with US Muslim communities to raise awareness of issues affecting Muslims. The CAIR website includes reports, surveys, public service announcements, and press releases on issues of specific concern to American Muslims and on Islam-related topics of general interest.

Federal Bureau of Investigation (FBI)
935 Pennsylvania Avenue NW, Washington, DC   20535-0001
(202) 324-3000
website: www.fbi.gov

The Federal Bureau of Investigation (FBI) is the investigative arm of the US Department of Justice. It investigates violations of federal criminal law; protects the United States from foreign intelligence and terrorist activities; and provides leadership and law enforcement assistance to federal, state, local, and international agencies. Press releases, congressional statements, major speeches on issues concerning the FBI, and crime statistics are available on the agency's website.

Manhattan Institute for Policy Research
52 Vanderbilt Avenue, New York, NY   10017
(212) 599-7000 • fax: (212) 599-3494
website: www.manhattan-institute.org

The Manhattan Institute for Policy Research is a conservative think tank that supports economic choice and individual responsibility. The institute publishes a quarterly magazine, *City Journal*, that advocates conservative, free-market urban policy. Many articles, interviews, policy papers, and reports written by the institute's fellows are available on its website.

**National Association for the Advancement
of Colored People (NAACP)**
4805 Mt. Hope Drive, Baltimore, MD   21215
(877) 622-2798
website: www.naacp.org

Founded one hundred years ago, the National Association for the Advancement of Colored People (NAACP) is the oldest civil rights organization in the United States. Its primary focus is the protection and enhancement of the civil rights of African Americans and other minorities. Working at the national, regional, and local levels, the organization educates the public on the adverse effects of discrimination; advocates legislation; and monitors enforcement of existing civil rights laws. The NAACP publishes *Crisis*, a bimonthly magazine, and provides press releases on its website.

National Urban League (NUL)
120 Wall Street, New York, NY   10005
(212) 558-5300 • fax: (212) 344-5332
website: www.nul.org

A community service agency, the National Urban League's mission is to eliminate institutional racism in the United States. It also provides services for minorities who experience discrimination in employment, housing, welfare, and other areas. It publishes the report "The Price: A Study of the Costs of Racism in America," the annual "State of Black America," and other reports.

US Department of Homeland Security (DHS)
Washington, DC   20528
(202) 282-8000
website: www.dhs.gov

Created in 2002 following the September 11, 2001, terrorist attacks on the United States, the Department of Homeland Security (DHS) serves as a coordinating agency providing information about potential threats to America and its citizens, as well as offers tactical options to take action and prevent further harmful events. Publications such as "Commitment to Race Neutrality in Law Enforcement Activities" are available on its website.

US Department of Justice (DOJ)
950 Pennsylvania Avenue NW, Washington, DC   20530-0001
(202) 514-2000

e-mail: AskDOJ@usdoj.gov
website: www.usdoj.gov

The mission of the US Department of Justice (DOJ) is to en-force the law and defend the interests of the United States ac-cording to the law; to ensure public safety against foreign and domestic threats; to provide federal leadership in preventing and controlling crime; to seek just punishment for those guilty of unlawful behavior; and to ensure fair and impartial admin-istration of justice for all Americans. Publications available on its website include "Guidance Regarding the Use of Race by Federal Law Enforcement Agencies" as well as articles about current DOJ activities and links to DOJ agencies such as the Civil Rights Division.

Bibliography of Books

Martha R. Bireda   *Cultures in Conflict: Eliminating Racial Profiling.* Lanham, MD: Rowman & Littlefield, 2010.

Michael L. Birzer   *Racial Profiling: They Stopped Me Because I'm—.* Boca Raton, FL: CRC Press, 2013.

David Boonin   *Should Race Matter?: Unusual Answers to the Usual Questions.* New York: Cambridge University Press, 2011.

Joseph Collum   *The Black Dragon: Racial Profiling Exposed.* Sun River, MT: Jigsaw Press, 2010.

Elizabeth Comack   *Racialized Policing: Aboriginal People's Encounters with the Police.* Winnipeg, Canada: Fernwood Pub., 2012.

Anthony Cortese   *Contentious: Immigration, Affirmative Action, Racial Profiling, and the Death Penalty.* Austin: University of Texas Press, 2013.

Alejandro del Carmen   *Racial Profiling in America.* Upper Saddle River, NJ: Pearson Prentice Hall, 2008.

Karen S. Glover   *Racial Profiling: Research, Racism, and Resistance.* Lanham, MD: Rowman & Littlefield, 2009.

Vikas K. Gumbhir   *But Is It Racial Profiling?: Policing, Pretext Stops, and the Color of Suspicion.* New York: LFB Scholarly Publications, 2007.

David A. Harris   *Profiles in Injustice: Why Racial Profiling Cannot Work.* New York: New Press, 2002.

Amaney Jamal and Nadine Naber, eds.   *Race and Arab Americans Before and After 9/11: From Invisible Citizens to Visible Subjects.* Syracuse, NY: Syracuse University Press, 2008.

Mareile Kaufmann   *Ethnic Profiling and Counter-Terrorism: Examples of European Practice and Possible Repercussions.* Berlin, Germany: LIT, 2010.

Cynthia Lee   *The Fourth Amendment: Searches and Seizures: Its Constitutional History and the Contemporary Debate.* Amherst, NY: Prometheus Books, 2010.

Heather Mac Donald   *Are Cops Racist?* Chicago, IL: Ivan R. Dee, 2003.

John H. McWhorter   *Losing the Race: Self-Sabotage in Black America.* New York: Free Press, 2000.

Gregory S. Parks and Matthew W. Hughey, eds.   *12 Angry Men: True Stories of Being a Black Man in America Today.* New York: New Press, 2010.

Marcos Pizarro   *Chicanas and Chicanos in School: Racial Profiling, Identity Battles, and Empowerment.* Austin: University of Texas Press, 2005.

Stephen K. Rice and Michael D. White, eds.   *Race, Ethnicity, and Policing: New and Essential Readings.* New York: New York University Press, 2010.

Stephen J. Schulhofer   *More Essential than Ever: The Fourth Amendment in the Twenty-First Century.* New York: Oxford University Press, 2012.

Jeff Shantz, ed.   *Racial Profiling and Borders: International, Interdisciplinary Perspectives.* Lake Mary, FL: Vandeplas, 2010.

Judith Sunderland   *"The Root of Humiliation": Abusive Identity Checks in France.* Ed. Benjamin Ward. New York: Human Rights Watch, 2012.

Carol Tator and Frances Henry   *Racial Profiling in Canada: Challenging the Myth of "A Few Bad Apples".* Toronto: University of Toronto Press, 2006.

Michael Tonry   *Punishing Race: A Continuing American Dilemma.* New York: Oxford University Press, 2011.

Ronald Weitzer and Steven A. Tuch   *Race and Policing in America: Conflict and Reform.* New York: Cambridge University Press, 2006.

Tim Wise   *Colorblind: The Rise of Post-Racial*
                    Politics and the Retreat from Racial
                    Equity. San Francisco, CA: City
                    Lights Books, 2010.

Brian L. Withrow   *The Racial Profiling Controversy:*
                    What Every Police Leader Should
                    Know. Flushing, NY: Looseleaf Law,
                    2011.

Index

A

ABC News, 57–58
Abdulmutallab, Umar Farouk, 61, 101, 112
Ackerman, Spencer, 108–110
Affirmative action
    definition, 37
    discrimination differences, 39–40
    problems corrected by, 38–39
    racial profiling differences, 37–44
    racial profiling similarities, 33–36
    racist discrimination and, 43–44
    slight impacts of, 40–41
Affirmative Action: Racial Preference in Black and White (Wise), 41
African Americans
    "all blacks look alike" syndrome, 130
    arrest of Robert Taylor, 22
    driving infraction inequalities, 156
    exaggerated reports about, 313
    excess actions against, 27–28
    North Carolina traffic stop study, 212–213
    stop-and-frisk interactions, 18
    SUNY Oneonta lawsuit, 181–186
    systematic harassment of, 95–96
    use of deadly force against, 179
    witness bias considerations, 130
Age profiling, 77
Airports
    Britain political correctness issues, 65–69
    Entebbe hijacking, 64
    Israel racial profiling, 61–62, 64
    profiling acceptability at, 34, 36
    San Diego airport incident, 85
    US profiling of Arab Muslims, 83–87
    US screening biases, 80–81
Al-Arabiya news channel, 72
al-Arian, Sami, 110
Alaska Natives, 177
Aldawsari, Khalid, 112
Allah, 109, 110, 113
"All whites/blacks look alike" syndromes, 130
al Qaeda, 67, 72, 110
al-Rashed, Abdul Rahman, 72
American Civil Liberties Union (ACLU), 26–29, 85
    comments on racial profiling, 120
    discrimination argument, 121
    Florida Highway Patrol report, 208
    SB 1070 legal challenge by, 190
American Immigration Lawyers Association (AILA), 190
American Indians, 177